Robert S. Barrett

Thought seed for holy seasons

Robert S. Barrett

Thought seed for holy seasons

ISBN/EAN: 9783337895112

Printed in Europe, USA, Canada, Australia, Japan

Cover: Foto ©Lupo / pixelio.de

More available books at **www.hansebooks.com**

FOR

HOLY SEASONS

BY

REV. ROBERT S. BARRETT

AUTHOR OF "CHARACTER BUILDING," ETC.

DEDICATION.

IT IS SOMETIMES SAID OF A MAN THAT "HE IS A GENTLEMAN
AND A SCHOLAR." IN THE FULL AND LITERAL SENSE
OF THESE WORDS, THIS MAY BE SAID OF MY
LOVED AND ESTEEMED FRIEND,

Bishop Dudley

OF KENTUCKY.

IT MAY BE ADDED THAT HE IS A
CHRISTIAN IN THE REAL MEANING OF THAT
GREAT WORD; AND A CATHOLIC BISHOP, TOO, IN THE
TRUEST AND BEST SENSE OF CATHOLIC. FOR THESE REASONS
THIS LITTLE BOOK IS AFFECTIONATELY DEDICATED TO HIM.

PREFACE.

THE CHRISTIAN YEAR, with its dear associations, with its tremulous memories, with its holy days and its marvellous story, awakens in every heart some thoughts and hopes and resolutions. A few of my own reflections I have here given you. They are but "bare grain," mere seeds gathered after the bloom has faded. Of the flowers which I have woven into the Christmas evergreen wreath, and the Good Friday thorn-crown, and among the Easter lilies, I have kept the seeds, and present them now to you. I pray that they may be suggestive of at least some part of the living thought and purpose of which these seeds are but a poor expression, and that God shall take this "bare grain," and give it a body, as it shall please Him.

THOUGHT SEED FOR HOLY SEASONS.

Advent Sunday.

WE instinctively believe in Judgment. We have a presentiment that wrong will be righted, that the crooked will be made straight, that justice will at last prevail. We believe in a Day, — it may be far off, — when the unequal chances of men will be considered, when the principle of judgment will be, "To whom much is given shall much be required," and men shall receive equal praise for equal fidelity. Perhaps the most despised thing in all the catalogue of Christian men is the ignorant heathen convert, who, in his blind and faulty way, is groping up to the light; yet at the eventide he may receive more — he will certainly not receive less — than the eloquent preacher who lays down the law for a multitude. It will be seen that it is as hard to crawl a rod through the slums of paganism, as it is to ride a mile on the highways of Christian civilization. Even among us, opportunities for doing good are uneven. There are rich men and poor men, dull men and clever men, sick men and well men. In the noble race of doing deeds, the unencumbered, independent, free and strong man comes first to the goal, and easily too. He is applauded. Last to arrive is the unsuccessful creature who has dragged along under the chains of poverty or the weights of disease. But the sweat of a greater effort is upon him. He receives no applause ; perhaps ridicule instead. But in the great cloud of witnesses is God. He sees the chains, the weights, the sweat, the greater effort, and He says, " Thou hast been faithful over a few things, I will make thee ruler over many things."

Second Sunday in Advent.

AN English newspaper assigns its editorial work to specialists. Lawyers write on law, soldiers on war, farmers on agriculture. One *editor-in-chief* selects these men and supervises their work. The paper has a great main object, but it gets at this object through many channels. It may be Conservative or Liberal, but it promulgates its principles among all classes of men. Merchants, mechanics, lawyers, physicians, are sure to find something of interest written by men of their own professions, and in language which they know. Thus the Bible has one great main object. It is "profitable for doctrine, for reproof, for correction, for instruction in righteousness." It is a book for every age and all the world. It has *many authors*, but it has *one Editor*. He selects men of every character and clime, every degree and occupation, and they do their work under his unerring supervision. Thus rich and poor, kings and peasants, poets, philosophers and fishermen do hear them speak in their own tongues the wonderful works of God. In David's poetry, in St. John's narrative, in St. Paul's logic, the Holy Spirit permits no omission, no error. In all this manifold flow of thought there is a oneness of editorship which declares that all Scripture is given by inspiration of God. Yet a book for sages and babes. Our blessed Bible! Its *divine* element grasping the wisdom of God, its *human* element dispensing it to the sons of men. An infallible depository of religious truth, within the reach of all capacities.

> " And he may read who binds the sheaf,
>   Or builds the house, or digs the grave ;
>   Or those wild eyes that watch the wave
> In roaring round the coral reef."

Third Sunday in Advent.

A S St. John the Baptist prepared the way for
the Christ, so God's minister prepares our
way for death and judgment. This prophet of
Jordan may be rough or sombre, this voice in the
wilderness may seem a solemn sound. Its soul-
searching directness may irritate, may anger us.
But we had better heed. Men almost instinctively
resent reproof; they do not like plain truths about
themselves. Light hurts weak eyes; honey burns
sore throats. Lais, the Corinthian beauty, broke
her mirror because it showed her wrinkles. This
is foolish. I ought to be grateful to any who help
me to know myself. When I remember how I
shrink from reproving another, I ought to feel
deeply indebted to the man who has brought him-
self to the point of reproving me. Some one has
said that no man can be perfect without either a
watchful enemy or a faithful friend. Let us value
the faithful friend. He may not tickle our van-
ity, as does the honey-tongued flatterer, who, like
Vitellius, worshipped Jehovah at Jerusalem and
Caligula at Rome, but he will make us stronger
and purer. The faithful friend may not be wise, or
even delicate, in his methods, but let us appreciate
his spirit. We, not he, will lose most if we drive
him from us. If fallen under a burden, would you
resent the service of him who came to lift it? If

wounded, would you repel the hand outstretched to set the broken bone? If benighted in the wilderness, would you take ill the proffers of a guide? Welcome, then, the true minister of God, who comes to lift the burden of sin, to heal the wounded heart, and guide your wandering feet back to the Father's house.

Fourth Sunday in Advent.

CONSCIENCE is a fact. You may disregard it, but you cannot deny its existence. You may disobey it, but you must listen to it. Conscience is not at our disposal. Its message is simple, but urgent. It says, "Do right, do right," — only this. It does not decide what is right. We must decide that for ourselves. We are responsible for our decision. Conscience is no casuist. It simply says, "Do right, do right." It is a voice within us, but it comes from without us. If we disobey, conscience whips us, and we must submit. The voice may be hushed for a time, but only for a time. Conscience may be smothered by passion. It may be trampled under foot by selfishness. Pride may take away its sceptre, pleasure may seize its crown, wilful sin may usurp its throne. But its voice will whisper, "Do right, do right." And by and by its revenge will come. Then it will no longer whisper. Passion loses its grip, selfishness, sin, and pride become impotent. Conscience arises in its wrath, seizes again its throne and crown, waves its sceptre over wreck and ruin, and cries aloud, with the voice of a victor, "Do right!"

Christmas Day.

PAGANISM is misplaced incarnation. Some of these fancied incarnations are very revolting, and some of them are really sublime. The Egyptian's cat and crocodile are gross forms for God to take. The horrid fetiches of the Dark Continent are even worse. The Greek mythologies are classic and beautiful. There is something imposing in the fire-worship of the Parsees, and the Indian's river-god moving in majesty. But when God did really come to dwell among us, He came as a human child, an infant in its mother's arms. This is at once the most mysterious, the most beautiful, and the most universal form God could take, as far as we can think. The most *mysterious*, because Darwin and Huxley acknowledge no more baffling mystery than that of mother and child. The most *beautiful*, because Raphael and Murillo attempted to paint nothing more beautiful than a child in its mother's arms. The most *universal*, because the

traveller who encircles the earth hears no voice
which declares the brotherhood of man like the
voice of an infant. It is a universal language,
always the same, whether the plaintive cry come
from the Indian pappoose hanging from the bend-
ing bow, or from the Italian bambino among the
sunny hills of Tuscany. The same one touch of
nature, whether coming from Laplander's furs, or
Hottentot's booth, or Hindoo's bungalow, or Turk's
kiosk, or Arab's tent, or the silken curtains of a
palace, or the squalid poverty of a garret. Mys-
terious! beautiful! universal!

Holy Innocents' Day.

NESTLE close to the warm heart of Jesus, thou
little one; for there alone among all the re-
ligions of the earth is a place for thee! Christ's
religion respects children. It considers nothing
else in all this world more worthy of respect and
love. Childhood is sanctified by the God-Child.
Our blessed religion looks upon children as im-
mortal creatures, full of beauty. They are the
inheritors of the kingdom of heaven. We are so
accustomed to see children treated as if they were
really people, that we do not appreciate the bless-
ing of it. It is by no means a matter of course

that children are respected. Look at the social
contempt in which Mahometan children are held.
Look at the random influence of the infidel's child.
The atheist may indeed treat his child after the
Christian custom of the land he lives in; but at
the bottom of his creed the child is a mere perish-
ing brute. Listen to the shrill shriek that comes
from the fiery altar of Moloch, and the splash on
the banks of the Ganges. Look at China's infant-
icide, and the blood on the Juggernaut's wheel.
Then look at Christendom's child enthroned, —
enthroned in the church, in the home, in the
school, in Christian art, and in the Christmas fes-
tival. Blessed be the Bethlehem manger, that
makes holy the estate of childhood. And God
bless every child and every childlike heart this
blessed day.

The Sunday after Christmas.

ONE very good thing about adversity is that it
makes us sympathetic. We feel *with* the af-
flicted as well as *for* them. And the afflicted real-
ize this, and that is the best part of it. If I am in
trouble there comes to me a friend who has never
known sorrow. I thank him for his well-meaning
words, but they do not get near my heart. Then
comes a woman in deep black; no words come

from the crape veil, but a soft hand is laid upon mine in silence, and the magnetic touch of sympathy conveys comfort from her life to mine. Thus God entered into all the conditions of human grief and weakness, not that He might feel *for* us, but that He might feel *with* us, that He might be touched with a feeling of our infirmities, and that we might realize this. He became all things to all men, to teach all men that sin was the only condition which his sympathy cannot touch. To the suffering, He is the Man of Sorrows; to the isolated, He is treading the wine-press alone; to the joyous, He is the guest at the feast; to the poor, He hath not where to lay his head; to the laborer, He is the carpenter of Nazareth; to the aged, He is descending into the valley of the shadow of death; to the boy, He is a boy; to children, and to all of us who have need to cherish children, He is the helpless babe nourished at a woman's breast.

End of the Year.

A LADY once dreamed that she was sailing in a boat, and that her necklace having broken loose, the pearls were dropping one by one into the sea, yet she could not prevent it. It is no dream, but a reality, that we have the bitter pang of seeing our precious years slipping from us forever, one by one. Oh, subtle, insatiable Time, what hast thou not devoured! The devourer leaves but little indeed, to him whose treasures are laid up on earth. At the year's end they have a handful of dust — memories, regrets, and worse. What a time this is to weigh the dust of the dead past! A poor creature in despair was heard to make the crazed cry, "If thou canst call back Time again, then there is hope for me!" It cannot be done. It is gone! We shall never see it again till the judgment. There is no use to follow along behind Time, with hot tears and vain regrets and moral sentiments. The proverb says, "Wisdom walks before Time, and Opportunity beside it." Turn your sentiments and tears into resolution, faith, and prayer. Make Time give instead of take. It will give you a sweet conscience and a happy hope. It will give you soul treasures which it cannot take away again. Time will be the vestibule of Eternity. The passing years, one by one, will be the successive upward steps to God.

Circumcision — New Year's Day.

SOMETIMES we stand by the open grave. The well-known form swings down in silence to its narrow bed. "Earth to earth, ashes to ashes, dust to dust." The men cast down the sod; the sexton smooths off the mound; the priest steps back; the spades and the ropes are laid aside; then comes one silently and puts down a wreath of roses, and another with trembling hand lays down a cross of chrysanthemums, and another with moist eyes comes with an anchor of evergreen, and the cold grave is covered with flowers. Ah me! It's a pity that all the flowers were kept till the friend was dead. Perhaps a single bud in the sick-room would have made one day less tedious. Perhaps a single mark of consideration would have lifted the burden and inspired hope. Who can tell? On this glad, this sad new year, let us remember that we have living friends and children and God's own poor. It will do them, at least, more good, if now, and not hereafter, we weave the wreath of roses for the pathway, or a chaplet of encouragement, or a cross of faith, or an anchor of hope.

Epiphany.

THE spirit of Christianity is getting away from self. The farther the better. The farther from self, the nearer the spirit of Christ, who came so far to die. There is much self in our kind deeds. In our Christmas gifts to friends there is much self-gratification; less in the gift to the parish; less still in the contributions to the diocese; less still in those sent to domestic missions; and least selfishness of all, and therefore more religion, in money sent to foreign missions. Jesus was the greatest foreign missionary. St. Paul was a true foreign missionary. There were plenty of sinners in Asia, but the command said, "Go into all the world." The foreign field was Europe. Think of that! Europe! And yet some question the success of foreign missions. Then, centuries later, America called for help. No doubt some said, " We have too many practical heathens at home." But others sent help to America. Now some here begrudge the pittance which goes to do for others what was done for us. They say, " Look at the poor and ignorant at home." Well, look at them by all means, and help them too. But do not take the little ewe lamb from the poor man's bosom to feed thy guest; take it from thy abundant flocks. Do not take the sparse trifle from the mission fund to teach the heathen at thy door. Take it from the abundance of fashion, from the millions devoted to luxury, from the fortunes lavished upon dissipation and vanity. Do God's command, and save thy soul. He says, Spread the gospel abroad. It will succeed; never fear. Of course much foundation work, costly masonry, must disappear before the superstructure gladdens the eye. But all true work is God's, and in his time the work will rise to sight, a splendid fabric, like Europe and America.

𝔉𝔦𝔯𝔰𝔱 𝔖𝔲𝔫𝔡𝔞𝔶 𝔞𝔣𝔱𝔢𝔯 𝔈𝔭𝔦𝔭𝔥𝔞𝔫𝔶.

HOPE is man's inspiration. Hope's yoke is easy, and her burden is light, and her toil is sweet; for with magic wand she inspires man with her pictures of the future. When the weary student burns the midnight oil, she keeps her vigil too, and paints the honors of commencement day. When she would wipe the sweat from the laborer's brow, she summons up the cheerful glow and domestic joy of a future hearthstone that shall be his. When she would cheer the fainting farmer's heart who sows his seed upon the upturned sod, she unfolds the fields of waving golden grain. When she would speed the caravan across the arid sands of the desert, she pictures the gurgling fountains of the oasis and the waving palms. When she would nerve the sailor's heart to climb the swaying mast, she portrays the prospect of the green hills and white cottages which encircle the placid harbor far away. When she would fire the soldier's blood amid scenes of carnage and death, she holds before his eyes the spoils and crowns of victory. Yes, hope is man's inspiration, his solace in trouble, his guide in perplexity, his strength in weakness; the poor man's wealth, the sick man's medicine, the belated traveller's lamp, the prisoner's window, the Christian's very life.

Second Sunday after Epiphany.

THERE are men whose religion is like a stringed instrument, that must be tuned before it will perform. Another's religion is like the human voice, always ready. There are men who pray without ceasing; that is, they keep in the presence of God, so that they can speak with Him at any moment. To such a man, prayer is the almost unconscious breathing of the soul. As the miser holds spiritual communion with his gold wherever he may be, as the ambitious man plots in silent thought, as the glutton craves his meat and drink, thus the prayerful man, whether he works or plays or travels, will feel beside him the solemn and sweet presence of God. This very sense of God's presence is prayer. Prayer is not something put on, something foreign to us. It is part of us. It is like a golden thread woven into a beautiful texture. It frequently disappears and reappears; yet it runs all through, beautifying and strengthening all. Let the golden thread of prayer be woven in among the many varied threads of our life, touching all, strengthening all, beautifying all.

Third Sunday after Epiphany.

" GOD is too good to damn anybody." So we
hear some say nowadays. They are quite
right. God does not damn anybody; but many
damn themselves. Damnation is sin and suffering
producing and perpetuating each other. We see
suffering producing sin in this world, and sin pro-
ducing suffering. Look at the low dens, with
their diseased, poisoned, putrescent inmates, their
depravity, their profligacy, their brutality, their
bodily torture, their mental anguish. Is not that
damnation? — sin and suffering acting and react-
ing. Hell is that same thing projected into the
soul's future. God does not damn men. He tries
to prevent it. He moves heaven and earth to
prevent it. Was not the crucifixion moving
heaven and earth? The crucifixion was God's
supreme effort to keep men from hell. How un-
reasonable to charge God with your death! Sup-
pose I went, sick and suffering, through the stormy
night to hold a light for you at some dizzy chasm;
suppose you struck down the light which I had
brought with so much pains; suppose you lost
your foothold and fell into the abyss below, could
I be charged with your death? Well, then, did
not God bring you light? Did He not with scarred
hand hold that light over your pathway? If you

reject it and fall, can you charge Him with your
death? No; oh, no! "This is the condemna-
tion, that light came into the world, and men loved
darkness rather than light."

Fourth Sunday after Epiphany.

WE pursue different roads, but the same object,
happiness! Kings sit upon their thrones,
diplomates mature their schemes, orators make their
speeches, poets sing their verses, merchants trade,
architects build and mechanics toil, but the ultimate
end of all is happiness. And yet happiness is
hard to reach. It is like standing upon some hill,
and looking at the mellow summer sunshine that
tints a distant hill; we go in search of it, but when
we reach that hill we find it gray and cold, and we
look back and see the soft light shining on the
spot from whence we came. One says, "Pleasure
is what I want," so he laughs, and then says,
"Heigh-ho!" That sigh is the dregs in the cup.
Another says, "Love will make me happy."
Novels, as soon as they get their heroes together,
write "Finis," and close the book. The rim of the
cup is sweet; they do not let us see the bottom.
Another says, "Wealth will make me happy."
They used to tell me that if I got to the foot of a

rainbow, I would find a bag of gold; well, many a man has found the bag of gold, but the rainbow of promise has vanished. Some think there is happiness in fame. Not necessarily. Like cracked bells in high towers, some lives in great elevation give out no melody or sweetness. I will tell you how to be happy: trust God! The wise man said that, after having drained every cup. After pleasures the most extravagant, and luxury unequalled, and wealth unlimited, and fame the most illustrious, he said: "Whoso trusteth in the Lord, happy is he."

Fifth Sunday after Epiphany.

"I SAY that is a bad report, my boy. Some did worse, it is true, but some did better. The reason why I say your report is bad is because it is below the general average, and therefore you helped to *lower* and not *raise* the general average." All of this I said to a boy who showed me his report. Then I went off into this line of thought: We ought not to defer our actions to public opinion, to conventionality, because the world's opinion is lower than our standard of right ought to be. Public opinion is *average* opinion. It is not the lowest; not the highest. It is mediocrity in morals and religion. No doubt the level of public opinion is getting higher; but it is never raised by those who follow public opinion. It is raised by the increasing number of those who live above public opinion, and who thereby raise the average. If we would better the world, we will do it, not by conforming to the average, but by living above the average, and thereby raising the average. This, it seems to me, is the very least that is to be expected of every Christian.

Sixth Sunday after Epiphany.

HOPE may be a flatterer; it may be a true friend. It may be a light unto my path, or it may be an ignis-fatuus to lure my feet to death. Many have been *saved by hope*, many have been *lost by hope*. When an Ohio-river steamboat was burned, a passenger was drowned by a defect in his life-preserver. The first thing I do on entering the stateroom of a steamer or ship, is to examine my life-preserver. I once found one with the strings so insecure that if I had trusted to it, it would have betrayed me. How dreadful to trust hope, to follow hope, to be lost by hope! It is not apt to be so with that hope which comes of trial, which grows out of discipline, which has its door in the " valley of Achor."

The trouble with joy-born hope, nurtured in sunshine and luxury and ease, — the trouble with such hope is that it is conceited. It looks to self and not to God. It is based upon a continuance of prosperity. These cannot always continue. All of its joy has come from the quiet and comfort of its own narrow life. Such hope is doomed to sure disaster. It is like the spider spinning his silken web out of his own bowels, and laying his beautiful geometrical plans, when one sudden sweep from a counter plan brushes the graceful spinner and his work into one black ball of dirt, in which we find his hopes have become his winding sheet.

Septuagesima.

MILTON'S Paradise Lost, Dante's Inferno, Doré's cartoons, the weird word-painting of the pulpit, dreadful fancy pictures of hell, — all of this cannot make us understand what it is to be lost. It was not to purgatory or hell that Christ went, but it was into this world of ours that he came to seek and to save the lost. They were here. To be lost is to get away from where we belong. The lost sheep, the lost prodigal, were wanderers. They were not dead, they were not in hell; but they were lost. The soul does not belong to sin and the devil; it belongs to God. And if you want to know how lost the soul is, then learn how far it has gotten away from God. That is the thing to know. Heaven and hell are incidentals. If you take care to be saved from your sins, to be brought back to the image of God from which you have wandered, heaven and hell will take care of themselves. Now, if you would know how lost you are, put your life, with all its selfishness and littleness, beside the life of Jesus; your motives by his, your thoughts by his, your heart by his. Try and see how far you have gotten away from the perfect image of the God-Man. He is the perfect specimen of man, of which the rest of us are ruins, it matters not how magnificent these ruins may be. He shows us a specimen of man who is not lost. The image of Christ will teach us more about the lost than Doré's cartoons could ever do.

Sexagesima.

THE devil, by some surprising ingenuity, has contrived to create the impression that religion is unmanly. Most men desire to be manly, and most profess to be. What is manliness? Some very young persons have imagined that it is manly to smoke cigars or swear. Others think manliness is physical perfection, — strength, agility, skill, endurance. Of course, it is a Christian duty to develop the body. Other things rule by strength, but the body rules by weakness. If we would govern our bodies, they must be strong and well. A sick, weakly body will surely rule us as a tyrant. But manliness is in the soul. Indeed, no quality can be called essentially manly in which the brute may excel the man. Feats of endurance, strength, and skill have been applauded as manly; but no man can lift as much as an ass, or swim as far as a goose. Quick resentment and stubborn conflict have been thought manly, but this would make the bull-dog manly. Manliness consists of four things, — unselfishness, truth, moral courage, and earnestness. The selfish man is not manly, though he be as strong as Atlas. The liar is not manly, though he be the laureate pugilist of the land. The moral coward is not manly, whatever may be his physical hardihood. The frivolous man cannot be manly, for his life lacks purpose and positive power. Now, all of these manly qualities find their highest development in the true Christian.

Quinquagesima.

MEN in these times seem unwilling to hear of future punishment. Hell is no longer a word for ears polite. They talk as if "a certain class of preachers" invented hell and kept it burning to enforce their precepts. I was in Naples in 1884, the year that cholera was epidemic. The Neapolitans accused the physicians of bringing the cholera. The physicians predicted it; they told the people that unless they cleaned up their city the scourge would come. They laid down rules and gave warning. So when the cholera came, the people thought the physicians brought it to intimidate them into washing themselves and keeping their back yards clean, so they threw stones at the physicians and drove them out of the city. These physicians had come to risk their lives for the ungrateful people who rejected them. Thus when preachers begin to talk of the scourge which will follow sin, the people — that is, some of them — begin to think the preachers are in some way responsible for this scourge. The preachers are assailed as cruel, fanatical, behind the times, and all that. Our Lord is a physician. He came and found the disease of sin and its fatal consequences here already. He did not bring them. He left his home to improve the sanitary condition of this world, to cleanse its filth. And in order to induce men to submit to his treatment, He warns them to flee from the wrath to come.

Ash Wednesday.

WHEREIN lies the reasonableness of fasting? It is bringing the body into subjection; it is a recognition that the body is a machine. The body is an important machine, God given. It is a dangerous machine, capable of destroying its owner. A good servant, a bad master. It is to keep the soul's mastership that we fast. The best fasting will have this distinct object in view. It will be done with intelligence and system. There is a vast deal of random, aimless fasting, well meant, but blind. Could we not have a text-book on fasting, — a book of tactics to increase our efficiency in fighting the flesh? For want of something else, suppose we use some book on hygiene. How would Dio Lewis on " Our Digestion " do for a guide to fasting? Why not have a competent teacher to tell us what to eat, how to eat, how much to eat; to tell us what food and drink conduce to animal development, what manner of living helps to bring the body into subjection, and make it a useful servant instead of a cruel master? If we have intel-

ligence and system about this important business
of fasting, it will be much more interesting, reason-
able, and helpful to us.   It will surely not be less
Christian or acceptable to God because it is done
with system, not less devotional, not less compati-
ble with prayer.   And these hygienic rules of life
will furnish ninety-nine out of every hundred per-
sons all the scope for abstinence from *food* which
they could desire, or which a season of humiliation
could demand.   Of course propriety will suggest
abstinence in other directions, — abstinence from
gayety and festivity while we are commemorating
the sufferings of our Saviour.

Second Day of Lent.

FORBIDDEN fruit is sweet.   It is sweetened
by the devil.   One forbidden tree in Eden
seemed better than a thousand trees allowed.   That
terrible magician has power to concentrate our gaze
upon one object — power to withdraw our eyes from
the pure and wholesome fruits of many trees, and
rivet them upon that one forbidden thing.   He so
intensifies our thought upon that one desire that it
outgrows all desires, and perhaps life itself for the
time seems stale and flat unless that one desire be
gratified.   That is one of the supernatural powers

of the serpent to charm his victims. This dreadful
delusion, this deadly fascination, fills common ob-
jects with dazzling beauty. The colored lights of
hell are reflected upon earthly things, and make
them appear heavenly. Thus the gaming table is
made to assume attractions which make money and
land and houses insignificant trifles in comparison.
Thus a glass of liquor grows in beauty and power
that will out-dazzle the love of family, or the joys
of home, or even the hopes of heaven.

Third Day of Lent.

WHEN the pot of passion boils over, then
human law takes cognizance, not before.
In this it differs from the law of Christ, which sees
the ingredients in the caldron seething, bubbling,
prevented only by fear from boiling over often.
Thus with murder, — the law sees it only in the
crimson blood and the ghastly corpse; Christ sees
boiling in the heart, the pot of death, the poisonous
ingredients of hate and greed. " Whosoever hateth
his brother is a murderer." So with adultery.
Society takes cognizance of the sickening scandal ;
but Christ sees the poison in the heart, sees the
fire burn, and the caldron boil, and the poison
seethe, and exultant demons, witch-like, join hands

around the charmed pot, and add their odious portions. Ah, human heart! wilt thou thus lie still and let devils brew within thee the hell-broth of infamy and death? Do you think, because no human eyes see this, that it is innocent or safe?

"Blessed are the pure in heart, for they shall see God." Aye, and woe to the foul in heart, for God shall see them.

Fourtß Day of £ent.

WHEN David proposed to build a house to God, his pious wish was appreciated, but God told him, through honest old Nathan, that he could not build the Lord's house. David's hands were bloody. God is in no hurry. He desired the temple to be built. He wanted it, but it had better never be built than to be built by wrong methods or wrong precedents, or by the wrong man. He told David that He had already been represented on earth by a tabernacle for centuries, and that He could wait. A transient resident of a miner's camp can live in a tent, but when a man is going to spend his life in a town he builds upon the best foundations, and adorns his home with the slow-growing and sturdy oak. Corporations build stronger, and governments stronger still. Historic churches are willing to devote centuries to the slow growth of massive minsters. So the eternal God would rather have his work done properly than quickly. He would rather have his work true and silent, than noisy and false. He would rather have it solid than showy; unseen and eternal rather than seen and temporal. He would rather have one Bible given away by a clean hand than ten distributed by a foul one. He would rather have five Christians who are Christians across counters, and over dinner-tables, and behind neighbors' backs, than a thousand who are Christians only in church on Sunday morning. He would rather have the Church grow with an increase of ten sincere conversions, than have it flooded with a hundred shallow professions, with its certain ebb-tide of ninety backsliders.

First Sunday in Lent.

"REPENT!" This word reverberated through the wilderness waste of Judea. "Repent!" This was the keynote of the Baptist's preaching. "Repent!" This caught the haughty Pharisee's ear, and startled the mailed Roman. "What shall we do?"—"Do?"—"Yes, what?"—"Do good." — "Is that repentance?"—"Yes." — Repentance is positive, tangible. It is not sentiment, it is not pretty words, it is not a spasm; it is plain duty, it is downright determination to do right, so help me God. This John preached, this Jesus taught. Repentance is not crying, " Lord, Lord!" but doing the will of my Father which is in heaven. Mercy, justice, humility, purity, truth, — doing these things, and the undoing of their opposites, that is repentance. To the slave of flesh, repentance means control; to the libertine it means chastity; to the stingy it means liberality; to the slanderer it means charity; to the harsh it means gentleness; to the impatient it means long-suffering; to the discontented it means gratitude; to the sinner it means that which he is not and ought to be. Of the incidentals to repentance — sorrow, tears, emotion — the Bible takes little account, because it would not divert our attention from the main thing, which is to hate sin and forsake it.

Fifth Day of Lent.

LAST summer the good ship *Wieland* brought over a large number of caged birds. When we were about mid-ocean one restless bird escaped from his cage. In ecstasy he swept through the air, away and away from his prison. How he bounded with outspread wings! Freedom! How sweet he thought it! Across the pathless waste he entirely disappeared. But after hours had passed, to our amazement, he appeared again, struggling towards the ship with heavy wing. Panting and breathless, he settled upon the deck. Far, far over the boundless deep, how eagerly, how painfully had he sought the ship again, now no longer a prison, but his dear home. As I watched him nestle down on the deck, I thought of the restless human heart that breaks away from the restraints of religion. With buoyant wing he bounds away from Church the *prison*, and God the *prison*. But if he is not lost on the remorseless deep, he comes back again with panting, eager heart, to Church the *home*, and God the *home*. The Church is not a prison to any man. It gives the most perfect freedom in all that is *good* and all that is *safe*. It gives him liberty to do what is *right*, and to do what is *wrong* there is no rightful place to any man in all the boundless universe.

Sixth Day of Lent.

LOVE! St. Paul eulogized it in his Corinthian Epistle. Love is the Christian's life, his rule, his motive power, his incentive, his destination, his reward, his God. Orators' eloquence, singers' melody, angels' songs, without love, are hollow, heartless sound. Theological knowledge without love

is dry lumber in a garret. Leo X. and Henry VIII.
were theologians. A man may have dogged faith
in a cause that will energize his will to move
mountains of difficulty, like Richelieu, yet without
love he is nothing. He may play the card of alms-
giving, and be defiant to the martyr's stake; with-
out love it profiteth nothing. Long-suffering and
kindness are its *general characteristics.* "Envieth
not"—let others be happy. "Vaunteth not itself"
—does not swagger and talk big. "Does not be-
have unseemly"—hate, not love, makes men do
ugly. A healthy parasite of hate growing at a
man's heart eats up all its sweetness. Love "seek-
eth not her own"—she is not forward; she is no
loud creature made up of paint and noise, but a
coy maiden, calm as the blue sky, modest as the
wee daisy, pure as the mountain rill, *Charity!* "Is
not provoked"—loseth not her temper. Con-
trolled temper is a splendid energy. Lose your
temper, and it will find you. "Thinketh no evil"
—instead of putting two and two together and
making four, it takes two from two, making nothing.
"Rejoiceth not in iniquity"—there are those who
rejoice in an enemy's disgrace, though hell triumph
by it. "Rejoiceth in the truth"—charity never
minimizes the truth. Love never says, "Oh, well,
it don't make any difference what you believe."
"Beareth all things"—like the broad sea, quench-
ing every spark of spite. "Believeth all things"
—believes in brother man with all his faults.

" Hopeth all things "— man will yet come to the goal with palms of victory. " Endureth all things "— love makes watching and waiting and toil sweet.

Seventh Day of Lent.

IN Mammoth Cave the old negro guide told us how people had been lost there from time to time. When found, they overwhelmed him with embraces and other demonstrations of gratitude. Some became insane through fright ; some fled in terror from the guides. Once a woman was lost for about twenty-four hours. In that terrible darkness, in the silence in which hearts beat loud, she had waited in dreadful suspense. Superstitious dread filled her crazed heart. At last the guide came, his footfalls echoing like whispers and groans, his lantern casting ghostly shadows upon the walls. The poor terrified creature arose, and fled away into the darkness. The guide pursued — a veritable black devil he seemed ! At last he overtook her,— unconscious, prostrate, ashy white. In his strong arms he raised her from the ground, and carried her out to safety and light and home !

How often is it so ! When the Saviour comes, we flee from him. Misconceptions of Him, distortions of Him, shadows of Him in this dark world, fancies of Him in our sinful hearts, make Him

seem other than He is. And we flee from our
Saviour and our Guide — flee away into the dark-
ness. And yet He came to find us, to save us, to
bear us to the light. He came to his own, and
his own received him not.

Eighth Day of Lent.

IT is said that man is a religious animal. He
must have some religion. To any Christian it
must be the religion of Christ ; that or none. We
cannot go back to paganism. We cannot return to
Judaism. Judaism is nothing but a promissory
note. If Christ is not the Messiah, that note is
two thousand years past due, and daily becoming
more worthless and more hopeless. We cannot go
to Mahomet, riding armor-clad and blood-stained,
leading us to a life of revenge and a heaven of sen-
suality. We cannot accept Brahmanism, with its
vedas and its Hindoo gods, with its metaphysical
quibbles and its social tyrannies. Every woman,
and every man with wife and sister and daughter,
says, we will have no Brahmanism. We cannot
be atheists, and say "There is no God!" for then
would Nature's heart cease to beat, and we could
only stand orphaned by its mighty corpse, and wait
without hope till we are buried at last in the same
eternal grave of rayless night.

Ninth Day of Lent.

THERE is no contrast so fearful as the contrast between the illusions of temptation before the sin is committed, and its reality afterwards; between the appearance of the forbidden fruit as it hangs upon the tree, and the taste it leaves in the mouth. How cruel the tempter's irony when he said, "Your eyes shall be opened"! No sooner had the hell-kindled desire been indulged, than their souls were smitten with a cold and shivering disgust. The fruit turned to ashes in their mouth. The tree so beautified by colored lights of hell dwindles to a thorn-tree, scattering seed to curse the soil and tear the children's feet. The angelic radiance of the tempter falls off, and betrays the cold coils of the loathsome serpent. The flowers of Eden wither as soon as plucked, and the garden itself is blasted and blackened by the fires of an outraged conscience.

Tenth Day of Lent.

HOW defective, how false, is the world's judgment! If the Pharisee labors and prays to be seen of men, verily he shall have his reward. He shall be seen of men, and praised of them, too, no doubt. But what is it all worth? Praise is the most hollow, the most uncertain thing. The enhancement of worldly circumstance makes men appear better than they are. What a veil will wealth throw over a rich man's vices! What attraction will beauty give even to the ignorance and folly of a woman! What undeserved applause merely accidental success will win! Wealth, beauty, genius, success, are pedestals upon which a moral dwarf may stand, and look taller than the moral giant who stands upon the plain earth of homeliness or poverty. But it will not always be so. "We brought nothing into this world, and it is certain we can carry nothing out." We will carry no pedestals out. When we stand before the judgment-seat of Christ, we will stand upon our own feet and be judged as we are. Then will follow the great reversal of human judgments. "Many that are first shall be last, and the last shall be first."

Second Sunday in Lent.

I REMEMBER with distinct vividness the most relished food I ever ate. It was a hard crust, by a mountain rill. The sauce was hunger. Again, a sense of duty has often made me go almost with loathing to a sumptuous feast. In one case each dry crumb turned to blood and

strength. In the other case each rich morsel
turned to lead and stupor. Let teachers of chil-
dren consider this. Well-meaning mothers or cur-
riculums may stuff without nourishing. Thus
some as full as a bookshelf are no wiser. God
feeds through the appetite. " He hath filled the
hungry with good things, and the rich hath He
sent empty away." Thus the pale, crammed grad-
uate, rich in self-esteem, sheepskins, and mother's
kisses, may go empty away, — empty of mental
vigor and clear vision. There are men full of
moral platitudes, and empty of moral principle ;
full of maxims, good forms, and Pharisees' formu-
las, but empty of real love for truth and right.
In religion especially thousands are starving, not
for want of food, but for want of appetite. What
has clogged your soul's appetite ? Perhaps it
needs fresh air. Then force your soul out of the
narrow walls of self. Perhaps it needs exercise.
Then grapple with some good and earnest Chris-
tian work. Perhaps it has been surfeiting on
sweetmeats. Then discard forever religious sen-
timentality — a religion of trash — newspaper, yel-
low-back-novel religion. Come hungry, and God
will feed you. " Blessed are they which do hun-
ger and thirst after righteousness ; for they shall
be filled."

Eleventh Day of Lent.

OUR Lord knows what is in man. The superficial, upper soil does not deceive Him. Under the covering of good clothes he sees the false heart if it be there. Under the careless disciple's dirty skin, he may see a promising life, if it were only washed. Christ saw through Judas and Herod and the Pharisees. He saw through Simon Peter. This Simon is at bottom a rock. There was considerable trash about the man, — impulse, inconsistency, and meaningless talk, — but a rock after all. Jesus looked to this at a glance. He did not discuss it; he saw it. he felt it, he knew it. This fine quality of mind, this delicacy, this sensitiveness which unconsciously photographs character with a look, usually belongs to the more subtile minds of women. It is a divine quality. Some men have it to a high degree. The Saviour had it to an unspeakable degree. His delicate sensibility, his perfectly sympathetic heart and mind, are as impressive as the conscious quicksilver to catch a faultless image of our life, our troubles, our fears, and doubts. His being in heaven does not impair his power to know us and sympathize with us. Therefore He is the true father confessor, the great priest, to whom we can go with assurance. We shall not be misunderstood. Like the mother's heart — far more than the mother's heart — will his instinctive love respond to each heart pang and fear.

Twelfth Day of Lent.

THERE is no description of heaven in the Bible.
Even what the Revelation of St. John says of
it may be regarded as symbolical. There are hints,
symbols, almost glimpses, but no description. The
Talmudists described heaven, and made it a gro-
tesque and ludicrous fairy-land, full of ogres and
giants. Mahomet described heaven, and made it
a magnified earth, full of magnified vices and sati-
ated sensualists. The Bible does not describe
heaven, because there is no use of describing it
to us, whose earthly capacities could not grasp it.
To our immature faculties it is indescribable. Let
a child see men, give him books about manhood
to read, yet he has no conception of the emotions,
the thoughts, the fears, and the hopes of a man.
Suppose a prophet could have described to Adam
the nineteenth century. I doubt if Gabriel him-
self could have made Adam understand the social
condition, the religious, the political, the mechani-
cal revolutions, of our day. So would it be impos-
sible for us to understand heaven, with its vast
social developments and its ritual splendors, with
its mighty, sweeping changes, with its growths
and evolutions, by which its perfected citizens are
ever progressing from glory to glory.

Thirteenth Day of Lent.

NATIONS must settle their differences by arbitration instead of war, because we have such commercial relations with our antagonists that we cannot afford to fight. For the same reason the differences between the Church and the world ought to be settled by arbitration, because of the close domestic, social, and financial intimacy between them. The Paul of the nineteenth century is a guest in Mammon's house, and Mammon publishes his sermon in the morning paper. Yet let us never forget that with all these appearances of peace there are two distinc' sides. The conflict is just as real, the victories are just as glorious, and the defeats just as ruinous, as though the conflict were a conflict of blood. This is the modern, the civilized mode of conflict, — the conflict of diplomates instead of armies, the conflict of pens instead of swords, of brains instead of brutal force. Let us remember that in this quiet conflict between God and Mammon, between truth and falsehood, we all bear a part. Let us not be deceived by the silence of things. Men are borne in silent flight to ruin upon the noiseless wing of hellish tendencies. Let not the moral savor of the world's philosophy hide from our eyes the hollowness and idolatry which everywhere surround us. We must conform to modern usage, it is better. Let the conflict be a moral fight. But we must never for one moment lose sight of its real and vital character. Let not the devil escort you to hell with a smile.

Fourteenth Day of Lent.

SOME persons have thought that the highest aspiration of a Christian's life is to get to the dead level of innocence. They measure their spiritual progress by the question, "How far am I from the devil?" instead of "How near am I to God?" But all of this is merely negative, not positive; destructive, not constructive. Some one has compared the religious life to moving into a house. There are repairs to be made. Perhaps the foundation timbers are rotten. But when the house is repaired it has still to be furnished, and we must furnish each one his own spiritual house. Every man is the cabinet-maker of his own soul furniture. We are the weavers to upholster our own hearts. We are the artists to decorate the walls of our own imaginations. We are the musicians to make and tune the stringed instruments that are to fill our lives with melody. If we are idle, our spiritual house will be empty and cheerless and musicless.

Fifteenth Day of Lent.

SHALL we prove that it is reasonable for a lawyer to practise law? for the farmer to sow seed? for the merchant to buy and sell? Shall we prove, then, that man should do that which he was made to do; that the creature ought to serve the Creator? This is his business. If he do not that, he is a failure as a man. Even as an animal his success is only partial. The deer is swifter, the ass is stronger, the sparrow is merrier. As a man he is a failure. He may be a success as a clothes-weaver, or as a fact-collector, or as a money-gatherer, but as a man, as a child of God, as a member of the kingdom of heaven, he is a failure. Like a book used for fuel —a failure as a book, and poor fuel. It is sad to see anything debased to low and sordid ends, which was made for high purposes. Here is the hulk of a noble ship, used for a wrecker's hut. What a fall was there, thou once fair and free-winged rover of the sea! Here is a goodly garden become a swine-pen. Miry filth instead of delicate and fragrant bloom. Here is a caged eagle with wing broken and feathers befouled, hobbling in the dirt. Ah, thou king of aërial heights and purity! But far sadder than all is the immortal spirit of man, bound by the habits and crippled by the passions of the world, — like the lap-wing, crowned with a crown, and feeding on dirt.

𝔖ixteenth 𝔇ay of 𝔏ent.

CHARACTER is a building of which every man is his own architect. Human characters present every variety, from the rickety hovel to the Gothic minster. Among great characters there is a wide diversity of style. There are Gothic characters, and composite characters, and Romanesque, and Oriental, and classic. We have the classic Parthenon, and Addison and Macaulay. We have the Roman Coliseum, and Martin Luther. We have the Stones of Venice, and Jeremy Taylor. We have Edinburgh Castle, and Thomas Carlyle. We have Westminster Abbey, and William E. Gladstone. We have the Pyramids of Egypt in their grand and enduring simplicity, and we have Robert E. Lee. John Ruskin tells us there are "seven lamps of architecture," or seven principles which must enter into every building that aspires to true greatness. These principles are sacrifice, truth, power, beauty, life, memory, and obedience.

It may be said that that character also is truly great in which John Ruskin's seven lamps of architecture find their highest development.

Let architects of material building study the Coliseum, where the three orders of Greek architecture are found, — Doric in the first story, Ionic in the second, and Corinthian in the third ; but let character-builders study the life of Jesus Christ, that temple in which all of John Ruskin's seven lamps of architecture meet in perfect proportion.

Third Sunday in Lent.

WATCH! Temptation comes as a whipped foe, and begins to say, "Oh, I am worsted; there is no danger in me." Watch it! Firemen watch the smouldering coals that the wind may again inflame. Men watch closely that place in an embankment which has once given away. Again, temptation comes with a new face, and says, "I am not your weakness." Take heed! Faithful Abraham lost his faith, meek Moses was impatient, . David became sensual, and lion-hearted Peter trembled. Again, temptation comes as a child, and says, "Oh, I am so little, I cannot do any-thing." Watch it! Little temptations are seeds of the upas-tree, eggs of the serpent, sleeping dynamite. The devil puts the little Oliver Twist through the window to open the door for him, the big robber. Hell is first lit with shavings. Again, temptation comes as a smiling friend, and says, "You know me and love me ; fear not." Watch it! The beloved Delilah betrayed the strong Sam-son to death. Watch and pray. The sentinel's power lies in his communication with the power that supports him, and then watchfulness. If he watch only, he can do nothing when the enemy comes. He is one, the enemy is an army. But if he too can summon an army, then is his watching effective. So is prayer the Christian watchman's communication with the powers above him. If he watch only, he can do nothing, for he contends with principalities and powers and spiritual wickedness in high places. But if he watch and pray, he, too, can summon powers omnipotent to his rescue. And prayer is communication with that Power.

Seventeenth Day of Lent.

SUPPOSE a boy should say, "It is great trouble to become a man. I must go to bed four thousand times, and get up and dress four thousand times, and eat twelve thousand meals, before I can be a man." We would think the boy foolish; we would say, "Let each day take care of itself." If our Christian duties become part of our daily life, we will never think of them as burdens. The joy and health of growth will repay us for all our efforts. Growth is its own reward. It is furnishing our spiritual house for eternity, it is tuning our harps for the harmonies of heaven, it is whetting the appetite to feed on angels' food. It is fitting ourselves for the presence of God. The growth of the soul never ceases. The body reaches its maturity and then decays, the mind arises to its zenith and then fails. But in the decrepitude of age the soul is in its youth. One of the joys of heaven will be its continued growth. God's children will not stand still there. Each year they will be better, each century stronger, each cycle happier than the last. Eternity will be one infinite approach to the glorious consummation, "Be ye perfect, even as your Father which is in heaven is perfect."

Eighteenth Day of Lent.

I HAVE read a story somewhere — I wish somebody would tell me where — about some men practising a strange revenge upon an enemy. They found him alone at a saw-mill deep in a forest. They bound him to the carriage of the saw, and, adjusting the carriage so that he would reach the teeth of the whizzing saw in about half an hour, they left him to his fate. With horrible suspense he viewed the bloodthirsty avenger, to which, inch by inch, he was drawn nearer and nearer. The savage foe shrieked, and its fierce teeth gleamed in the light. The prostrate victim at last seized this faint hope, — perhaps, oh! perhaps, the teeth of the saw would cut the rope and release him before it killed him. And so the suspense became more intense as he was drawn nearer still, and the supreme question became, "Shall this dreadful assailant be my deliverer or my destroyer?" Surely such a position of suspense and peril, such hazard, such jeopardy, is bad enough to be the revenge of the most cruel enemy. But the man who trusts to death-bed repentance voluntarily places himself in this terrible position. He wilfully places himself in a position where it is uncertain whether death, the great avenger, will be his deliverer or his destroyer. He wilfully places his soul in this situation of suspense and jeopardy. Nearer and nearer his soul draws on to meet the dreadful problem.

Nineteenth Day of Lent.

ONE of the most offensive features of atheism is that it takes away a man's treasure, and gives him no substitute. It robs him without equivalent. It merely destroys. Sometimes it is good to destroy. If we "pluck a thistle to plant a flower," if we destroy a den to build a school, if we take a half error out of a man's heart to make room for a whole truth, — that is good. But wanton destruction is cowardly and base. The destroyer, what a despicable creature! The whole brood of them is to be despised, from " the aspiring youth who fired the Ephesian dome," down to the Puritan iconoclast who robbed Scotland of her Gothic splendors. They are to be despised, and they are to be challenged. When one comes to destroy, have a guaranty from him; make him give bond that he will give better than he takes. Destruction requires no greatness, no courage, no genius. The low-browed vandal could destroy the creations of a Phidias. The fanatic caliph Omar could lay waste the literary treasures of Alexandria, the patient work of centuries. All honor to the builder! Away with the despoiler, the devastator! Challenge all who come with critic's scalpel and iconoclast's hammer. This is a safe rule in religion — safe in anything.

Twentieth Day of Lent.

MANY men spend their lives building foundations upon which they never erect any superstructure. They spend their lives preparing to live, and about the time they get ready to live they die. "I must have a fortune," says one; "life is not worth living without that." He forsakes society, he cramps his life, he has time for neither books nor friendship nor religion. These by and by. But his wife dies, his children marry and depart, and when at last he is ready, he finds himself without friends to reward or enemies to punish. Another will not begin life until he has great learning. But when, at the last, his arsenal is filled with ammunition, he awakes to find that the enemy has captured his territory. Lawyers despise real cases which they have, because they are dreaming of large cases which they have not. Some neglect a good practice for a precarious political career. Physicians, as a rule, settle early to real life, but even some of them make one feel that he is being used as a physiological study, to prepare the doctors for future usefulness. There are preachers with whom the country parish is a stepping-stone to the city parish, and the city parish is a blind from which to hunt a bishopric. That is wrong. Live in the present. Life is not far off. We are in it, perhaps near the end of it.

Twenty-first Day of Lent.

THERE are many men who consider God an object of charity, and his Church and ministers beneficiaries. They say, " Oh, I should like to give something, but it is all I can do to meet my regular expenses." Now, what I wish to emphasize is that *God is not an object of charity*, and religion *is* one of your regular expenses, whether you meet it or not. You might just as well get flour and

butter at your grocer's, and send your children to
school, and receive the attentions of a physician,
and protection from the government, and when the
grocer and the physician and the tax-gatherers bring
in their bills, say. " Oh. I should like to give you
something, but it is all I can do to meet my regular
expenses." You cannot get rid of the obligation
by staying away from church, for the beneficence
of religion is so far-reaching that even the scorner
is compelled to occupy the unamiable position of
receiving benefits from the very hand that he spits
upon.   •

Twenty-second Day of Lent.

THE entering wedge of the prodigal's ruin was
a wish — a wish for unhallowed freedom, an
unhallowed wish for what is only God's, — absolute
independence. This was the prodigal's sin. It is
the crying sin of a prodigal and wayward world,
this claiming legal right to license. this claiming
legal right to selfish. unrestrained, irresponsible
use of God's loans. — life. time. strength, intellect,
culture, beauty, money. Men crave to be gods;
but independence of God does not make men gods,
it makes them devils. This is just what made the
first devils. The angelic sons of God wanted free-
dom, and the Father let them go, and they left the
heavenly home and became prodigals and wanderers

forever. God's service is the most perfect freedom. It affords the largest amplitude of range, wide enough for the freest and boldest wing to fly. Its very limitations are intended for protection against other bondages, that are cruel and ruinous.

Fourth Sunday in Lent.

"HOME guards to the front!" was the cry of '65. Look at them, slight lads stooping under their heavy muskets, decrepit men tottering on with cane in one hand and gun in the other; convalescent, furloughed soldiers rising like a wounded war-horse. And has war come to this? Yes, and worse. It has seen the nursing mother, and feeble aged women, and delicate girls, defending the parapet. The hearth must be protected, and the husband, the little lad, and the white-haired father are gone, dead, dead in their blood! Women are to the front only because there are no men, none at all. But wait; there is a war for home and fireside, a war for rights more dear and from foes more cruel, in which women face its fury, not because the men have fallen first, but because men shirk. Yes, men shirk the discipline, the hardships, the responsibility of this war. Not all men, thank God! yet many do. Happy in their homes, receiving the blessings of Christianity, they are will-

ing to see the wives and mothers fight the battle.
The hosts of hell, with black flag unfurled, sur-
round us, menacing the peace of home, threaten-
ing slavery and death.   With dreadful malice and
cruelty they contend for every inch of ground.   It
is a battle, remorseless, ceaseless, momentous.   It
appeals to all that is manly in men to take their
places in it, to submit to its discipline, to endure
its hardships, to shoulder its responsibility.

Twenty-third Day of Lent.

"OUR Father which art in Heaven."   God is
more than a "great first cause," more than
an "inscrutable power."   He is a Father.   He is
a heavenly Father.   He is our Father.   Nothing
could be more reassuring; for "behold what man-
ner of love the Father hath bestowed upon us, that
we should be called the sons of God."   In all the
Bible invitations to prayer, there is none so encour-
aging as this: "If ye, being evil, know how to
give good gifts to your children, how much more
shall your Father."   Every fatherhood takes its
meaning and derives its beauty from the Father-
hood of God.   Every home circle is a likeness of
the heavenly home, of which God is the centre.
He is the Father, and his is the family after whom
"every family in heaven and earth is named."

This broadens our charity and deepens our humanity. Not "my Father," but "our Father," — mine and Jesus Christ's and Mary Magdalene's. From such a Father I look for sympathy, instruction, correction, and to Him I owe reverence, dependence, obedience, and imitation, — aye, and fraternity with all the children of God.

Twenty-fourth Day of Lent.

"HALLOWED be Thy name," we say. How can we? How can we hallow that which is already perfectly holy? How can we increase what is infinitely great? We cannot. But this we can do. Suppose on yonder wall were hung one of Raphael's paintings. We could add nothing to its marvellous beauty, but we might remove obstructions. We could improve the light, we could give glasses to the near-sighted, we could point out beauties to the untutored. So with God. We cannot give power to Him who has strewn space with worlds. We cannot extend the existence of Him who is from everlasting to everlasting. We cannot increase the wisdom of Him who paints every flower and guides every star. We cannot enlarge the providence of Him who

> " Throws open the golden gates of day,
>   And draws around a sleeping world
>   The dusky curtains of the night."

We cannot make Him more merciful, who gave his life a ransom for many. But this we can do. We can use our tongues and our lives to throw light upon this wondrous picture. We can remove the obstacles of worldliness and sin which prevent ourselves and others from seeing it. We can earnestly labor to educate the hearts of the untutored to feel its beauty, its glory, and its power. In this way we may hallow the name of God.

Twenty-fifth Day of Lent.

"THY kingdom come." The provinces of God extend through heaven and earth and hell. "Thy kingdom come," is a fervent prayer that all wrong shall be righted everywhere. It is a prayer for the militant Church, — that mighty army which, in weakness and strength, in success and failure, sets its banners against the powers of darkness and death. It is a prayer for the protection and development of the Holy of Holies, that Church within the Church, that invisible real within the visible nominal. It is a prayer for the Church triumphant, that the day soon may dawn when "He shall have put down all rule and all authority and power, and deliver up the kingdom to the Father, that God may be all in all." Thy kingdom come, O God, to shorten the day of death, to drive darkness from the earth, and, like the rising sun, dispel the deeds and fears of night!

A myriad voices, from a myriad lands, in a myriad tongues, seem to say, " The kingdom of God is at hand." Even so, come, Lord Jesus, — come quickly.

Twenty-sixth Day of Lent.

"THY will be done." The commander lays out his plan, and every mysterious order, every seemingly useless march and countermarch, every hard-fought battle, every apparently cruel execution or heartless act, every diplomatic measure, subserves to develop this plan, and bring it to its issue. So with Him " who ruleth over all." He has his plan. Every mysterious providence, every evolution of nature, every suffering saint, every ebb and flow of the Church's life and fortune, secretly but surely brings that plan to its perfect consummation. In this Divine Will we may be cheerful contributors, or compelled and unwilling agents. In the triumphant procession of God we may, we must, take a part, either by swelling the chorus or by following the chariot-wheels in captive's chains. " Thy will be done," is the cry of acquiescence. Submission does not mean insensibility. Grace makes the heart more tender. Those who submit most patiently suffer most

keenly and feel most deeply.   When the Christian
mother, in the silent hours of night, sees in fever-
ish dreams her dead babe near her still, and, wak-
ing, finds the pillow empty, we thank God that
she can weep.   Tears are God's gift.   Among the
gems of the Bible are the tears of Job and David
and Jesus.   Submission is seeing, through our
tears, the merciful hand of God.

Twenty-seventh Day of Lent.

"GIVE us this day our daily bread."   *This* day
implies regular and constant prayer.   *Bread*
implies the necessities, not the dainties of life.
Daily bread implies present needs, not future
accumulations.   *Our* daily bread means that the
channel of God's gifts shall be our own efforts.
Give us, means that though we plant and water,
God must give the increase.   Give *us*, not give
me, means that we must live and *let* live.   He
who can say all of this prayer is a happy man.
He has settled in his own heart the problem of
bread, for which the socialist is demanding a solu-
tion.   He has armed himself against discontent.

I have read of a child whose destitute mother
was trying to shelter it from the winter's blast.
They had gotten in a stack of straw, and were
fortunate enough to find an old barn door, which

they had pulled over their dry nest. As the sleet
and rain beat upon the door, and the wind howled
through the dark night, the little one snuggled
close, and putting her hand to her mother's cheek,
for she could not see her, she whispered, —

"Isn't God good, mother, to give us this warm
bed to-night? and aren't you sorry, mother, for the
poor people out in the rain and the dark?"

Ah me! let us learn, in whatsoever state we
are, to be therewith content. Hid in the hollow
of his hand, we shall be sheltered from the storm-
winds of all overwhelming evil.

Twenty-eighth Day of Lent.

"FORGIVE us our trespasses, as we forgive
those who trespass against us." Jesus
preached a sermon on this. In the parable of
the forgiven, unforgiving servant, He gives us a
picture of the impudence and hideousness of
unforgiveness. It is a strong, vivid picture, that
frightens us, and we exclaim, "Lord, is it I?"
There are some men — poor fellow-travellers to
the grave — whose step is so different from our
step that we cannot walk with them. But, surely,
there is no fellow-servant in sorrow, in sin and
in weakness, whom we cannot forgive from the
heart, while every day and hour we must crave

pardon from his Father and my Father, from his King as well as mine. Unforgiveness is disowning the mother that bore us free-born sons into the light and liberty of pardon. Refusing to forgive is like clambering upon some good rock to save myself from the angry sea, and then refusing to assist, refusing even to permit, another struggling mortal to climb upon it, claiming it as our right.

There is still another picture which Jesus has given us, which is the very climax of all that can be said or thought on the subject of forgiveness. After years of persistent persecution, misrepresentation, hatred, abuse, and insult, He watched his triumphant, intolerant enemies drive the nails through his quivering flesh, and prayed, " Father, forgive them, they know not what they do."

Yet He never had need to ask forgiveness for Himself. We must every day.

Fifth Sunday in Lent.

" LEAD us not into temptation." This petition comes naturally after the prayer for forgiveness. When a man wakes up to see hanging over him the spectre of sin, — unable to move, almost losing breath under the oppression of guilt, — he cries aloud, " Forgive, oh, forgive ! " When, then, the Lord comes to rescue him, to remove the weight, and he arises a free man, and catches a full breath of God's forgiveness, his first impulsive wish is that he shall not get into the same distress again. After the prayer "Forgive," comes the prayer "Lead us not into temptation." This is a terse and striking way of saying, "Father, lead us, lest we fall into temptation."

Give thy heart to God's leading, and the devil will keep out of the way. Keep the ear of thy conscience sensitive, so that thou mayst hear the still small voice saying to thee, "This is the way, walk ye in it." Go when grace calls thee, and where it directs thee.

Christian perfection lies in this: first, to skill the conscience to hear the Spirit's gentle voice, and then to obey. In all thy ways remember Him, and He will direct thy paths. Father, lead us, lest we fall into temptation.

Twenty-ninth Day of Lent.

"DELIVER us from evil." What disaster hath the devil wrought! What a train of evils! The daily newspaper is the record of the world's sin and sorrow and tragedy. What instances of depravity; what depths of hellish lust; what horrible murder; what sickening accidents; what

heart-breaking want; what sin; what crime! No
man can tell what a day may bring forth. One
begins the day in prosperity, and ends it in despair.
The sun rises upon a family with fair promises of
peace, and sets on their broken idols. A mother
kisses the red cheeks of her buoyant boy in the
morning, and at eventide kisses the cold lips of
his corpse. To-day our hearts swell with pride,
to-morrow our heads bend in disgrace. You
say this is pessimistic. Be it so. But all of these
things happen every day. God in his mercy grant
that they may not happen to us! Deliver us from
evil! Whether this evil mean the Evil One, or his
evil work, is not worth discussing. One is but
part and parcel of the other. All evil comes from
sin, and all sin comes from the devil. God deliver
us from them all!

Thirtieth Day of Lent.

DE PROFUNDIS! "Out of the depths have I
called unto thee, O Lord." These are the
words of some unknown but true poet. It is a
prayer; short, direct, intense, coming from some
heart of godly power; not rhetorical, but eloquent.
Not wreathing to the heavens like blue smoke to
be scattered by the winds, but ejaculated from
some rebounding soul, long bent, it pierces the
sky like an arrow. This is a voice, unknown yet

human, crying from the depth of some divine despair. Our hearts respond to its pathos. We know that it is not a perfunctory prayer that comes from the depths, but a cry. Afflictions give fervor and boldness to prayer. Affliction makes men earnest. Affliction is faith's element; as the life-boat which decays upon the shore and in the sunshine, triumphs on the breast of storms. I believe that every true Christian can look back over the past, and see in the depth of some great darkness, the memory and light of a fervid prayer, shining like a star. And the influence of such a prayer is never lost. Having once looked from the pit into the face of God, we can never wholly forget Him. It is our Gethsemane prayers that bring the angels.

Thirty-first Day of Lent.

OH, the life and strength and hopefulness and joyousness and buoyancy and exuberance of youth! We are young but once. We can have but one springtime. Springtime is the time for flowers, but it is also the seedtime. We would not like to see a young farmer who feels no pleasure when the first trailing arbutus breaks through the snow, or whose heart does not bound when the chirp of the robin first falls on his ear. But we think it will be all the sweeter to him if the flower greets him as he rides through the woods to his work, or if he hears the bird's morning hymn as he walks behind his plough. So will the flowers and songs and loves of youth be sweeter when they come in the intervals of labor, and among the purposes and efforts to do something good and worthy of strong young manhood. Youth will never come back to you, but you will carry much of its light and joy with you through life. Your summer, your autumn, and even the winter of your life, will be ever bringing forth the stored-up fruits of a well-spent springtime.

Thirty-second Day of Lent.

WE ought to encourage whatever increases or preserves reverence among our people. We are in danger of being a nation of iconoclasts. With unholy hands men tear down the monuments of the past, and nothing escapes their insatiable curiosity. They tear to pieces whatever is lovely, as the botanist tears in tatters the beautiful flowers, or as the smith melts in his crucible the graceful vase. God forbid that the spirit of inquiry should cease! Let it go on. Yet is not this dissection, this analysis of everything, in danger of destroying the romance and poetry of life? But you say, " Better truth than poetry." May we not have both? Is there any reason why the practical man should not have a soul, or why the scientist should not have a human heart? What I am speaking against is that unnatural insensibility, that affected *sang-froid*, that dry-eyes-and-cold-heart utilitarianism, which says that emotion is weakness and reverence is womanish. They are thoroughly practical. The splendid cathedral is a waste of money; Niagara is a mere water-power; Mammoth Cave is a mushroom garden; the Rhine is a steamboat canal; the Alleghanies are obstacles that ought to be dug down; the galleries of genius ought to be converted into factories; the performance of profound symphonies is a time to giggle and talk; friendship is a relic, and love is a dream, — this is what I protest against.

Thirty-third Day of Lent.

" There are more things in heaven and earth, Horatio,
Than are dreamt of in your philosophy."

STAND in a church spire. It has four windows, looking north, south, east, and west. From one we see the ocean, from one the city, from one the fields and farms, from the other the mountains. I once stood in a dome, with different colored glass in each window. Thus four men touching each other might see each a different scene; a red

ocean, a green city, blue fields, and yellow moun-
tains. A rare man might climb to the top of the
dome, and see the whole circle of the landscape
under the white light of a pure atmosphere. But
most of us look through one window, each upon a
different world, each world colored by our own
individuality. Four men in one street-car buy
the morning papers. A moment later one is read-
ing the editorial on politics, another the quotations
of the cotton market, another the society column,
another a report of a Sunday-school convention.
Four men sitting side by side, and each living in
a separate world. One man not dreaming of many
things in heaven and earth that are the very life
of other men: one looking upon the sea of com-
merce; another upon the fields of agriculture;
another upon the city of Vanity Fair, not dream-
ing of the Celestial mountains. They are there,
however.

Thirty-fourth Day of Lent.

THE walls of the great palace at Versailles are
covered with paintings of battles. The Bastille,
Jena, Austerlitz, the Pyramids! Agony, passion,
and death! Heroism and victory! One grows
weary with the endless profusion of art. He sits
down at last on the casement of a little window.
He looks out. Here, too, is a picture. Peaceful

France, with its green grass, its forests and fields, and its church tower beyond the placid lake.

The book of Ruth is such a little window amidst the historical pictures, the battle pieces of Israel. Through this window we see the home life which the pictures have hidden — godliness, unselfishness, love and peace. Is it not well for us to turn from the historic, the heroic, and, through some rift, take a swift, sweet glimpse of the pastoral and domestic scenes of life? We read of Sisera's murder and Jephthah's vow and Samson's revenge, and we think ill of Israel. Ruth gives us another view and a truer view. It is not for books and newspapers to publish what is ordinary and commonplace. They publish the remarkable, the wonderful. The very fact that a matter is publishable, is fair evidence that it is exceptional. Let us remember this. Let us remember that little Ruth is the rule, and not the exception. Thus, we will think better of Israel and of all the world.

Sixth Sunday in Lent.

THERE have been times when the drama was used as a moral and religious power. A crime enacted before them may have such an effect as to make the beholders absolutely safe from the committal of that crime. It is morally impossible for

one to do that for which his soul has conceived a
thorough revulsion. Thus were the angels of God
permitted to witness the historical drama of sin
and redemption. They were free moral agents.
They could fall, as angels had fallen before. But
they became spectators of this mighty tragedy. It
unfolds and progresses scene by scene. and act by
act. They see the ravages of sin, — Eve's tears,
Abel's blood, Sodom's flames. Disease, suffering,
and death reign. Depravity, abandoned and shame-
less, holds high carnival. The plot thickens. The
Son of God comes down : the shadows of the cross
fall over the scene ; pride, ingratitude, and hate
reject the God of gods : the heartless earth drinks
His blood ! All these scenes the angels see. Their
holy minds are filled with dismay, with aversion
and heart-sick loathing of sin. Though free
agents still, there is no longer even a possibility
of another rebellion in heaven. If, then, this
tragedy upon the stage of this very earth pro-
duced an ineffaceable impression upon the intelli-
gences above. what an influence for piety and
purity should it have upon us, for whose happi-
ness and welfare this divine drama was permitted
to be enacted ?

Monday before Easter.

I HAVE heard a criminal speak of his mother, and his lip quivered like a child's. Mother! Who gets beyond the power of that word? Who forgets his mother? What face in the medley picture of the past is so venerated as hers? Who weeps over our sins and misfortunes as she does? What heart feels like hers? Whose hand soothes like hers? Whose voice sinks to softer tones? Can you match her fidelity, her patience, her prayers? In the darkened sick-room, in the descending shadow of death, at the lonely grave, oh, my mother, there is no soft step, no tender eye, no warm tear like thine! To say, then, that the Church is my Mother, is to say all. She takes me at my birth. She places upon me a diadem; the jewelled drops from the baptismal font sparkle on my brow. She teaches me the form of sound words. She·vows me to a holy life. She feeds me with angels' food. She puts in my hand the trembling fingers of my bride. She watches over the changes and chances of my life. She keeps her vigil through the painful hours of my illness. Her words of supplication go up to God with my departing soul. She meets my pale body and bears it to the grave. And ever, year by year, she cheers my bereft ones with songs of immortal hope. Oh, my Mother, how could I live in this sinful, sorrowful world without thee? Oh, holy Bride of Christ, I love thee, I bless thee, I thank God that He has sent thee to love me, and bless me, and to be my Mother!

Tuesday before Easter.

WITHOUT Christ, hope is the falsest will-o'-the-wisp that ever lured to death the fainting soul of man. Men and women with hearts, think of a world without Christ! No Christ, and your mother's aged feet totter into a remorseless grave, from whose darkness no ray shines. No Christ, and the golden heads gathered around your knee are forced away forever by death's cold hand ere long. No Christ, and your own life is a quick transit, marked by successive birthday milestones —out, out into the starless deep. No Christ! Think of it when crape hangs upon the door and light goes out of the home. No Christ, and to whom shall the burdened widow go, and the down-trodden and the weary and the heavy laden? To whom shall dying eyes be turned? Without Christ, what is sweetest and most beautiful in so-cial and domestic life is lost. Eliminate Him, and what must you do? Tell the rosy, white-robed child to prattle its pretty prayer at your knee no

more. Close the Sunday-school and hush its joyous
anthems. Hang the Christian harp upon the
willows, with its " Rock of Ages " and " Jesus,
lover of my soul." Clasp the Bible, the dear old
book ; abolish the Lord's holy day; demolish the
churches, those beautiful sermons in stone ; speak
no words of cheer to the dying ; utter no tender
words of hope at the grave ; place no Christian
symbols on the coffin — no resurrection wreath,
no anchor, no crown ; efface the sentiments of an-
ticipation from the tomb. No Christ! Then the
heroism of Christian history from stake and dun-
geon is a pitiable lie ! No Christ ! Then " might is
right," will be the world's law, expediency its
morality, blasted love its present portion, and
death eternal its certain doom.

Wednesday before Easter.

" THE headstone of the corner " is a keystone.
A keystone is the wedge-shaped stone which
keys or binds together the sides of an arch at its
top. There is an ancient story that the temple-
builders, in absence of the architect, threw away
a keystone because of its peculiar shape. It would
not fit anywhere in the walls. Finally its proper
place was found, and it was raised to the top of
the arch. " The stone which the builders rejected

became the head of the corner," the keystone of
the arch.   A beautiful illustration, frequently
used, of the rejection and exaltation of Christ.
The rejection adds lustre to the glory.   Every
rejection of Christ turns out the same way:
whether rejected by Caiaphas, or Nero, or Herbert
Spencer, or Paris Commune, He is ever found, ever
raised, ever placed higher in the fabric, the head-
stone of the arch.   He has no other place.   He
fits nowhere else.   He is not one fine stone along
with the rest, Confucius, Buddha, and Mahomet.
He is the keystone, different in kind from the rest.
This or nothing.   His place is at the top.   The
whole fabric of history holds Him up to view.   He
binds together the arch.   Without Him the arch
must fall in.   Without Him the arch is an unsolved
problem.   He is the keystone, He solves the prob-
lem and locks the arch.   He is the keystone of
history.   Previous history comes up to Him on one
side, and subsequent history on the other side, and
He unites them.   He is the centre of history.   He
is the keystone of religion.   Religion is the arch
which bridges the chasm between heaven and
earth.   The arch, the bridge, cannot be complete
without the keystone.   The God-man touches each
side: his divinity touches the heaven side, his hu-
manity touches the earth side, and the arch is
completed, the bridge is effected.   **Heaven and
earth are brought together.**

𝕿𝖍𝖚𝖗𝖘𝖉𝖆𝖞 𝖇𝖊𝖋𝖔𝖗𝖊 𝕰𝖆𝖘𝖙𝖊𝖗.

WHEN the earnest Christian kneels at the altar to take the consecrated cup, he performs a sixfold act. It is an act of obedience. "This do!" Not a suggestion merely, not a time-honored custom only, but a command — explicit, emphatic.

> "Ours not to reason why,
> Ours not to make reply,
> Ours but to do or die."

It is also an act of remembrance. Not that Christ needed a memorial, but that we needed a memory. A remembered face may go with a child through life, to smile upon his virtues and weep over his vices. Memory is an angel — sometimes an angel with drawn sword. "In remembrance of Me." This is light for the pathway, this is strength for the soul. The holy communion is an act of thanksgiving — a eucharist. This is worthy. Nations honor themselves in honoring their heroes. Thus Garibaldi is honored in Italy, Luther in Germany, Napoleon in France. Thus Italy and France and Germany and all Christian people honor the world's Hero, the world's Saviour, in this sacrifice of praise and thanksgiving, in this eucharistic feast. It is also an act of fellowship — a communion. We join with angels and archangels and all the company of heaven and of earth to magnify the glorious name of God. It is an act of testimony. Every celebration of this sacrament is one new link in the continuous chain of testimony that comes down through the ages from the upper chamber of Jerusalem. Every hand that takes this bread and cup joins hands with the unbroken chain of priestly hands that reach back to the pierced hands of Jesus. It is an act of expectancy. We show forth the Lord's death till he come. We look back, and we look forward "till he come." It is going up to the altar on the mountain-top and looking to the eastern sky to see if there be any sign of the coming dawn.

Good Friday.

"THE precious blood." St. Peter calls it that. Once that blood had seemed to him more ghastly and hideous than shed human blood ever seemed before. Now it is precious. No other word describes the tenderness which he feels when he thinks of the blood of Jesus. He says, " Ye were not redeemed with corruptible things as silver and gold, but with the precious blood of Christ." Redeemed! A man is overtaken by misfortune. In deep distress, in dire necessity, he pawns a little gem that once adorned a loved hand now clasped in death. He creeps back day by day to see if his treasure is still in the window. He toils and pinches, until at last one day he puts down the hard-earned coin that buys back his treasure. Redeemed! Redeemed means bought back, reclaimed, the lost found, the dead alive again. We are redeemed; but not with corruptible things as silver and gold. If gold could have redeemed us, God would have turned a thousand suns into furnaces and cast the gold from a million worlds into their burning bosoms, and poured a molten river at the feet of Justice. But Justice demands the blood. "Without the shedding of blood there is no remission." God gives the blood — precious indeed; doubly his own. Is your child's blood soaking on the battlefield a precious price for liberty? This blood on Calvary is the blood of the Son of God. Is the governor's pardon precious to the prisoner in the dark, damp dungeon? More precious far is the blood-bought ransom that sets free the sin-bound soul. Does the sick and penniless prodigal seize with eager joy the pass that bears him back over the wide sea to his home? More precious still the covenant of blood which bears the soul over cold death's dark waves and admits him to his home with God.

Easter Even.

WHAT a power negative may have! Eye
hath not seen, nor ear heard, nor heart con-
ceived, what God hath prepared for those who love
Him! How expressive that is! What hath man's
eye not seen? What beauty? We have seen our
own fair-haired boy sleeping in the moonlight; we
have seen Niagara's rainbows, and the Jungfrau's
snow crown; we have seen the sleeping Como
waked by the coming dawn and blush. But eye
hath not seen it! — What hath ear not heard?
What melody? We have heard the warble and
chirp and trill, the matins of the fields, and the
evensong of the woods; we have heard, borne on
memory's wing, the dear, sad voice of the loved
and lost; we have heard the waves clash their
timbrels, and the wind's bugle blast, and the deep
cadence of the sea. But ear hath not heard it! —
What hath not the heart conceived? What power
and pomp of wealth hath it gathered in its imagin-
ation! What scenes of pleasure, what ecstasies
of love, hath it seized with its fancy! But neither
hath the heart of man conceived the things which
God hath prepared for those who love Him. May
we all love Him more and more.

Easter Day.

CHRIST was the Son of God when He was spit upon by slaves, but who could believe it? He was the Son of God when bleeding upon the cross, but who could realize it? The resurrection declared His Sonship. " He was declared to be the Son of God by the resurrection from the dead." Then the sun which had been shining behind clouds burst forth to sight. Man's heart revives at the sight. He rejoiceth in the manifestation of the Son of God. Of course it was not possible for Christ to be holden of death. But man did not know this. His death seemed to end all, to quench all light. The fond hope " that this had been He which should have redeemed Israel " was resigned with a despairing heart. Nothing short of the resurrection could have restored their confidence. Nothing short of this could have refuted the charge, " Himself he cannot save." Only the resurrection could have sustained men's belief in Him as a Saviour. But the resurrection declared Him to be the Son of God, and brought back the sunlight to men's souls. It decorated the Church's altars with the opening flowers of hope, and filled her mouth with everlasting songs. It sent the Church Militant marching on to meet the Church Triumphant. It discovered to the eyes of faith the incorruption and glory and power of the spiritual body; and to the eyes of hope, the day when our vile bodies shall be changed and made like to Christ's glorious body. It turns the sombre awe of the Mosaic Sabbath into the holy joy of the Christian Sunday, and changes the Babel tongues of sectarian variance into the Easter anthem, sung in unison, "Christ the Lord is risen to-day!" And both Sunday and Easter become foretastes of that blessed day which shall bring to pass the saying that is written, "Death is swallowed up in victory."

Easter Monday.

"MARY!" the word was pronounced by lips that had once been closed in death. May we not hope for as much in the future? Again those accents so familiar, so characteristic, will fall upon our ear. Our name shall be spoken, and then the reality, great and joyous, of eternity's unbroken love will fill our souls. Like Mary at the sepulchre, we shall forget the angelic forms about us, while with bewildered rapture we drink in the melody of a well-known voice which calls us "son" or "daughter," "brother" or "sister," "husband" or "wife," "father" or "mother" or "friend." Well may we sing anthems and chant Te Deums upon Easter Day, for it teaches us that our cemeteries are but the vast bed-chambers of sleepers who shall wake with the morning. This is the day which proclaims that God, who made man out of dust, will again raise the dead dust into living and familiar forms. This is the day which declares that we shall again touch the vanished hand, and hear the sound of a voice that is still, and the tender grace of a day that is dead will come back with all of its good and none of its evil; with all of its gladness and none of its grief; with all of its love, and none of those things which in this world frequently make love so cruel, so heart-breaking.

Easter Tuesday.

AS the dying seed becomes the plumed and fruitful tree, as the mouldering chrysalis becomes a winged and radiant creature, so our vile bodies shall be changed and made like unto Christ's glorious body. Our bodies! "These eyes shall behold, and not another." Bodies very different, yet identical. I have the same body that once lay a chubby babe asleep in its cradle. This is the same body that shall totter, weak and broken, to the grave. And it is the same body that shall stand before the judgment seat of Christ. The material particles ever changing, the identity ever unquestioned. Marcus Aurelius had five Christians burnt — a bishop, a deacon, a physician, a slave, and a child. He mixed their ashes and threw them into the sea. But Marcus Aurelius cannot frustrate God. The Creator can gather up particles whence he will, and clothe the living, self-conscious, undying soul with its own body, perfected and spiritualized. When God says, " Come again, ye children of men ! " then will they come. The sailor from the coral reef, the soldier bleaching on the desert, the martyrs' dust, shall not be forgotten then. The ashes which Marcus Aurelius mixed with the waters, the dry dust from marble urns, the mummied dead from vault and pyramid, the men of olden time, prophets and sages, kings and warriors, David and Saul, Pilate and Judas, Peter and John, Nero and Marcus Aurelius, Luther and Hugh Latimer, you and I, will be there.

First Sunday after Easter.

LIKE a coronation crown robbed of its jewels, so is the Gospel divested of the divinity of Christ. It is true there is pure gold left in the moral teaching and the matchless precept, but gaping cavities show where once the chief glory shone. Nor is the Gospel alone mutilated by denying the divinity of Jesus. The character of

Jesus as a man is brought down from a calm, consistent teacher, to a sincere, insane enthusiast. From divinity to insanity! that is an awful descent. But there is no alternative. Not only is the Gospel and the character of Jesus mutilated by a denial of his divinity, but my relation to Him is desolated. I find that I cannot touch the divinity of Jesus without touching my respect for his person. I might respect Him if He were a prophet like Moses or Elijah, or if He were a hero like Charlemagne or Luther. But as one who made the claims that He made, as one who demands my whole heart and my adoration, I must give Him that or nothing — or at most a tear. Without Christ's divinity my life's light dims, my love chills, my hope fades, the sunlight dies out of the spiritual landscape and all things lose their clearness in the universal shadow.

Second Sunday after Easter.

AT our birth our bodies become a battle-ground between life and death. During the first ten years death makes many conquests. At ten years death begins to fall back. At twenty life is triumphant. At thirty life foresees the future. At forty the battle is hot. At fifty death inflicts some wounds and life begins an orderly retreat.

At sixty life feels her strength failing. At seventy the retreat becomes a rout. At eighty death waves the black flag and cries, " No quarter ! " This is no fancy picture. It is no preacher's dream. It is a fact undeniable, inevitable, universal ! Indifference cannot affect its certainty, and scepticism cannot refute its truth. There is only one other fact with which we can confront this fact of death, and that is the resurrection of Jesus. Here fact meets fact. That is what we demand. We want a fact, a case, an instance, one single instance of resurrection. Once a sea-captain found his crew on shore apparently dead. The surgeon took one of the men and applied remedies, and the poisoned man stood on his feet. The captain shouted with joy, for in that one risen man he saw the possibility to save them all. So Christ brings life and immortality to light. His resurrection is not metaphysics, but history. Not a speculation for the future, but a fact of the past. Not a problem to be solved, but the solution of all problems.

Third Sunday after Easter.

AT the completion of an arduous work we assemble to commemorate the glad event. Magnates and officials meet to drive with great *éclat* the last spike which completes a great railway system. Owners and makers gather together

with flying flags to launch a mighty ship. When
the great work of world-building was done, when
man, the last crowning creation, was evolved, when
all was inspected and found to be very good, the
Triune Creator commemorated the completion of
the stupendous work by observing the first Sabbath
day.

It was not until thousands of years after this
that this commemoration was on Sinai crystallized
into a law. Thousands of years again rolled by,
and this Sabbath was superseded by the Christian
Sunday. The Sabbath commemorated the comple-
tion of the work of creation; Sunday commemo-
rates the completion of the work of redemption.
And as redemption is greater than creation, Sun-
day is greater than the Sabbath. You ask, Can
any work be greater than creation? What wisdom,
what goodness, what power are seen in the devel-
opment, the unfolding, the ever-opening plan of
creation! The persistent on-going of the universe
to the strains of "upward and onward." Yet re-
demption is greater. For God could sit upon his
throne in joy and wave up with the wand of
omnipotence the successive stages of the world's
development. But in the work of redemption He
got down from his throne, got down to the form
of a servant, got down under the heavy cross, got
down to the dust of death. Oh, it was an arduous
work even for the Omnipotent One. And when
the Easter morning dawned at last; when Christ

came up from the place of departed spirits; when
He came up from the last hard effort of his great
and completed work, the Church, unbid, but with
a universal impulse, said: We will rest with our
Saviour; his Sabbath shall be our Sabbath; it is
the Lord's Day, and it shall be our day forever.

Fourth Sunday after Easter.

HAVE you friends whither you go beyond
the sea? You leave good friends behind;
they watch your frail bark descend the pathless
main and sink below the ocean's rim. But, on
that strange and distant shore, who awaits your
coming? Acquaintances, relatives, familiar forms
have gone before you. But are there any there
who are safe and happy because you helped them
heavenward? Are there any who have a smile of
recognition and a hand to welcome you, as one of
the holy influences that bore them to that shining
shore? Have you helped to save a soul? Have
you used this fleeting world, this unrighteous
mammon, to make spiritual friends, who, when
you fail in death, shall receive you into everlasting
habitations?

Will a winged seraph meet you with the cry,
" I am the poor man whom you welcomed to your
pew"?

Will a radiant cherub hail you, poor ship-wrecked sailor, as "my beloved Sunday-school teacher"?

Will a sainted spirit clasp your hand and say, "I am the outcast whom your sisterly sympathy led to the Magdalen's Saviour"?

Will some humble worshipper say to your trembling soul, "I am the agnostic whom you showed God by your godly life"?

Will some white-robed chorister say, "I was the blasphemer whom you taught reverence"?

Would still another, "I was the drunkard whom you reformed"?

Welcome! welcome! to the everlasting habitations! The original has "everlasting tents," a beautiful allusion to the dear old tent life of ancient Israel, glorified and perpetuated in the eternal future. Welcome! welcome to the everlasting tents! And if in wonder you exclaim, "What authority have you to receive me thus, and who is he who gave you this authority?" then shall the Son himself advance from their midst and say, "Inasmuch as ye have done it unto one of the least of these my brethren, ye have done it unto Me."

Fifth Sunday after Easter.

IT is a matter of small importance how a man dies. If he is prepared, if he is a Christian, it matters not how he goes to his crown. There have been some triumphant deaths, some wonderful deaths, before which the gates of Paradise seem to swing open and flood them with light, and the superior splendor of the invisible turned the dying hour into the souls' nuptials. Such were the deaths of St. Stephen and Polycarp, of Latimer and Payson and Hervey, and of some known to you and to me. But such angels' visits to the dying couch are few and far between. Most souls go out in clouds or storms; in unconsciousness or pain. But what does it matter? The only sinless soul that ever descended the valley of the shadow of death cried from the Stygian darkness and solitude, "My God, my God, why hast thou forsaken me?" But in that hour he conquered. He vanquished death and robbed the grave of its victory. What does it matter, then, if we follow Him through the darkness to the light, through the battle to the triumph? What does it matter if I tremble? Underneath me are the everlasting arms. What does it matter if I cannot see? He is leading me through the ebon shades. What does it matter if I seem alone? He goes with me as He has gone so often with others before, through what seem the untrod solitudes of death.

My feelings do not help me much, and my fears cannot hurt me at all. I am not borne to safety on the feeble wings of my own emotions, nor am I hindered by those

> " Spectre doubts that roll
> Cimmerian darkness o'er the parting soul."

The last hour of the laborer's summer day may be hot and weary, but the rest of eventide will be sweet, and the night will be cool.

The last mile of the homeward journey may burn the traveller's bleeding feet, but love and welcome will soothe the pain, and wipe the pilgrim's brow.

As we approach the land, the winds may be boisterous, and the waves break loud upon the rocky coast, but the harbor will throw its protecting arms around the home-bound ship, and we shall be safe.

The last charge of the battle may be the bloodiest and the cruelest, but it brings the victory and the peace.

The fury of disappointed fiends may be the most desperate, and their last assault upon my escaping soul the fiercest, but it is the last; it is the last. " Let me die the death of the righteous, and let my last end be like his " — an end of pain, of tears, of sin, and of death.

Ascension Day.   •

IN public, in the daylight, on holy Olivet, the
Lord finished with glory the career which he
began in obscurity.　He finished his earthly ca-
reer, but not his human life.　His ascension per-
petuated his incarnation.　He did not evacuate his
human body, but carried it with Him to the right
hand of God — with its nail prints and its thorn
scars.　Touched with a feeling of our infirmities,
our great High-priest has passed into the heavens.
There He ever liveth to make intercession for us.
With his pierced hands He is able to save to the
uttermost them that come unto God by Him.　He
is able to lift them up to the place where He reigns.
This gives place and locality to heaven.　Heaven
is somewhere.　It is where the holy feet of Jesus
stand, and, therefore, where the weary feet of his
pilgrims may rest.　It is where his lips, which
left the earth pronouncing blessing, still speak,
and, therefore, where the happy ears of his saints
may hear his blessed words of love and wisdom;
where loving eyes behold Him, the chief glory of
that glorious place, and the fairest object.

His own voice, speaking a welcome, will be
sweeter music than the seraphs' song.　What a
thrill it brings to the soul when one first beholds
Niagara, or Mont Blanc, or Westminster's towers,

or St. Peter's dome! How the heart quickens when the eye first sees some world-famed man — Gladstone, or Bismarck, or Tennyson! But to think, oh, to think, we shall see Jesus — his eyes, his lips, his hair, his hands! Even the thought throws us upon our knees; but the reality! — The ascended Lord! The Divine Man! The Everlasting Son! The King in his beauty! God help us all to be faithful.

The Sunday after the Ascension.

WHEN Christ ascended to heaven, there was far away from the quiet scene of Olivet — far away, and indifferent to Him, a flourishing and beautiful city. In the soft air of Italy, on the purple waters of the southern sea, Pompeii pursued her elegant tastes and luxurious pleasures. A little later, while St. John was yet living, this fair city was caught by Vesuvius, as a beautiful butterfly would be caught by a child, and preserved for future times. Pompeii was not destroyed, it was preserved. The cloud of penetrating ashes hermetically sealed it up, and perpetuated all of its glory and all of its shame. So that while Jesus is the same in heaven, we have also on earth a city which remains as it was while He was praying on Olivet. This is wonderful! Stand here this sum-

mer's evening while the sun is going down over
yon rippling sea.   Deathlike silence broods over
the vacant houses and the empty streets.   The
ruts look as if wheels had yesterday polished
them; the pavements as if but yesterday busy feet
had worn them smooth.   Here are mills and
shops, theatres and temples, schools and homes —
all vacant, all voiceless.   On ruin and wall, and
silent street, one reads, *Vanitas Vanitatum* —
written as if by the hand of God.

Beyond is the avenger, Vesuvius, lifting his
haughty head into the blue sky, indifferent to his
work of ruin, smoking his mighty pipe, and puffing
the clouds over the lovely valley.

There is something more startling still.   The
subtile ashes have made a death-cast of all that
lived in Pompeii in that fatal August of 79.
Here is the dove upon her nest.   Here is the
house-dog in the attitude of struggle.   Here is the
slave in the agony of death.   We see a soldier at
his post; a woman who lost her life trying to save
her jewels; a mother endeavoring to save her
children; and here a beautiful youth and lovely
maiden kneeling hand in hand, where the grim
priest, cloud-robed, wedded them forever and forever.
As we gaze upon these relics of the hoary past,
how little does it seem to matter, when a new form
is unearthed, whether it be a slave or a prince,
a soldier or a lover.   The great question is, was
he a Christian?

Whitsun-Day.

THE Third Person of the Trinity. A Person, not a thing; not a function, not an influence; but a Person. He creates; He gives; He commissions; He instructs, strives, grieves. Not it — He! The Witness, the Comforter, the Sanctifier. By what touching symbols the Bible describes him! He is as free as water, and as refreshing. As illuminating as the light. He is as searching as fire, and as purifying. As reviving as the air. Powerful as the wind, and as mysterious. He consecrates like the oil that consecrates a king. Like oil he heals. He is as imperceptible as the dew, and as fertilizing as the rain. He is as gentle as a dove. He warns like a voice. He gives security like a seal. Mr. Herbert Spencer may not know him, but to the true Christian heart he is more real than Mr. Spencer is. He " bears witness with our spirit that we are the children of God, whereby we cry, Abba, Father." The Holy Spirit and Herbert Spencer agree in this : that " the natural man receiveth not the things of the Spirit of God, for they are foolishness with him, neither can he know them." He is as unknowable to the carnal eye as light is intangible to the blind eye, or music to the deaf ear. But to the new-born soul, to the soul that has received wisdom from the

omniscient Spirit and help from the omnipotent
Spirit, the denials of the blind agnostic excite only
compassion.   Christ sent Him to take his own
place in this world, and He is as real to the Church
to-day as the fair form of Jesus was real to the
multitude upon the mount or to his faithful
followers on the Sea of Gennesaret.

Whitsun-Monday.

I THINK the greatest check upon the abuse of
the body, upon intemperance, gluttony, or
licentiousness, is that God-inscribed sentence,
"Your body is the temple of the Holy Ghost."
Even bad men shrink from sacrilege, from a prof-
anation of what is holy.   The temple consecrated
to God, set apart by solemn services and devoted
to sacred purposes, excites emotions of reverence
in even hardened hearts.   Its sacred ornaments
and holy vessels are protected from harm by their
consecration.   He who robs a church or profanes a
temple is scorned by even the wicked as a sacri-
legious monster deserving no pity.   All feel the
impropriety of frivolity in a holy place and the
brutality of him who disregards the sanctity of
sorrow or holiness or purity.   Desecration of what
is holy, prostitution of what is noble, are de-
tested sins.   "Your body is the temple of the

Holy Ghost." If thou wouldst keep thyself pure, inscribe that divine sentence upon thy heart. Let it gleam there like God's handwriting upon the wall, which, indeed, it is. Let it burn like a signal light of danger over every scene of riot that would tempt thee.

Whitsun-Tuesday.

UNDER the power of the Holy Ghost the Christian conscience has reached, one by one, the successive planes of practical charity, each higher than the last. Since Jesus illustrated with the Good Samaritan that mankind is man's neighbor, and the earth is his neighborhood, gradual upward progress has been made. Since then every hospital, every orphan's home, every Magdalen's house of mercy, every missionary society has been wrought into living form by the Christian principle of brotherhood. And there are planes still to be reached. This principle will conquer the world for Christ. Its work may, like the coming tide, come with many a receding wave, but it will come at last. The last shackle will be struck from the last slave. The curse of drunkenness will disappear from human habitations. The tyranny of money will be restrained. The sufferings of the poor will be alleviated. Heathen idols will be turned to stepping-stones, pagan temples to schools. The shrines of superstition will be abandoned. Grim-visaged war will smooth his wrinkled front; and a Christian world, united by bands of steel and bonds of trade into a common neighborhood, and cemented by the Saviour's love into a common brotherhood, will hail the white-winged Peace!

Trinity Sunday.

NATURE cries out for a Creator; History cries out for a Redeemer; Conscience cries out for a Sanctifier. — Thus we have already a presentiment of God before we open our Bibles. When the Bible reveals the Triune God, Nature, History. and Conscience cry in chorus. "All hail!" The Bible is full of a Trinity. Through its web there ever runs the warp of Unity, into which is woven, strand by strand. the blessed Trinity, making more clear the beautiful garment of God. The Bible begins with a Trinity: " Let us make man " — let us, not let me — "let us make man in our image." Make man a trinity; make him intellectual. emotional. volitional, three in one. But the Trinity means something more than merely three aspects of God — as, for example, the three phases of the moon. It is rather like the sun, which is one; and the light and color and heat of the sun, which are three. The essential elements of Christ's manhood dwelt in God long before his incarnation by the Virgin; as the white ray dwelt in the sun before it was incarnated upon the cloud through the virgin rain-drop's lens. How strange that any should attribute this doctrine to Athanasius! Suffering saints sang it in the Gloria in Excelsis a hundred years before Athanasius was born: "Thou only, O Christ, with the Holy Ghost, art most high in the glory of God the Father." It has been sung ever since by Christian men of every name. It is interwoven through the ritual splendors of Rome and St. Petersburg; into the liturgic beauties of Canterbury; into the Puritan simplicity of Princeton. It has survived ritual changes and the shifting modes of thought and work, as some great cathedral stands unchanged in an ancient town where all else has been swept away by successive waves of war.

***

First Sunday after Trinity.

WHO made God? That is a foolish question. Is it more foolish than your question, "Who made the world?" Certainly. Why? Because we did not ask our question until we first proved that the world was made. If you can show that God was made, then you may ask who made

Him. The mind does not demand a cause for every existence. It only demands a cause for every change. To use the words of science, " We can go back to the era when the earth was a whirling ball of vapor, or when the sun itself was a giant nebula from which as yet no planet had been born." Now we have our fair earth with its organic life, with its blushing flowers, with its eagle's flight, and its William E. Gladstone. Here are great changes. Who wrought them? " The fortuitous concourse of atoms ? " That sounds very fine. but it means simply chance. Could chance, with even the help of all geological ages, bring a ball of vapor up to this world with its Shakespeare and its Jesus Christ? Could atoms blindly drift and eddy about into an intelligent and organized world? Never. Lord Bacon said that he " would rather believe in the fables of the Koran and the Talmud than to believe this." Christianity requires reasonable faith, but atheism requires unbounded credulity. Carlyle says of atheism. " One might call this the most lamentable of delusions, not forgetting witchcraft itself. Witchcraft worshipped at least a living devil, but this worships a dead iron devil." The fool hath said in his heart, There is no God. A man may study " sedentary crustaceans " for nine years and still be a fool.

Second Sunday after Trinity.

ANTHROPOMORPHISM! What a word! It means giving human attributes to God. Your over-sensitive infidel makes a great hue and cry over this. No doubt it has wrought harm. It has made God seem a magnified man, infinitely remote from the earth, intermittently revealed by some violation of law, intermittently accessible by the turn of the ecclesiastical wheel. But the harm has been done by thinking that these anthropomorphic descriptions of God were literal. Think of them as symbolic, and they are good. They **are** necessary. Whenever a thing gets beyond the grasp of our conception, whether it be a heap of coin, or geographic extension, or the infinite God, then we begin to speak of it in symbols. Much religious language and very much Bible language is purely symbolic, like the mathematician's equations or the astronomer's signs. Yet this symbolism adequately represents God to us. Because we know God better than we can speak of him. We know God directly. If we have no innate ideas, we have a God-knowing faculty. Cultivated, this faculty grows in strength and subtlety. Neglected, it will weaken and die. It will become atrophied by disuse; and we shall be like the eyeless fish of Mammoth Cave, that grope their way through the dark waters of their Echo River, while the blessed light gladdens the earth with its enswathing kiss.

Third Sunday after Trinity.

DOES not the intelligent design of the world overwhelm us with the personality and intelligence of what Mr. Herbert Spencer calls "the Power which the Universe manifests to us"? "He that made the eye, shall He not see?" The eye was made in darkness, yet it was made for the light. Was it not made by one who knew the light? Did not He who formed the ear in silence know the music and the sound for which the ear was made so perfect? If I realize that a knowledge of music is helping me the more to appreciate the works of Wagner, may I not infer that Wagner was a musician? If the increase of knowledge and science helps a Kepler or a Cuvier to appreciate the works of creation, may I not conclude that the Creator was a knowing and a thinking God? Shall not the Author of thought think? Shall not the Giver of life live? Is it not certain that in all these things, the eye, the ear, the brain, the heart, the idea precedes the realization? "In thy book were all my members written when as yet there was none of them." But when we speak of design, we are confronted with claims of mal-adaptation. But these are, no doubt, part of God's great plan. They are but the receding waves in the flood tide. Is not evolution itself the magnificent movement of a mighty drama developing under the hand of

God? Is not this unceasing, irresistible, upward movement the most complete, the most moral, the most religious argument from design for the unity, the goodness, and the intelligence of God?

Fourth Sunday after Trinity.

CONVENIENCE is no word for a Christian's mouth. It is a word of suspicious character. Convenience kills Christian enthusiasm and chills noble impulses. In matters of principle, convenience has no jurisdiction. In matters of religion it should never be consulted. There is no such thing as a convenient season for serving God. The lover might as well suspend his sighing, and wait for the course of true love to run smooth; the politician might as well content himself to wait in obscurity until all opposition withdrew; the engineer might as well sit down by his transit, and wait for hills to sink and rivers to run dry; the statesman might as well wait for the day when all political problems and all social knots untie themselves; the soldier might as well sheathe his sword until all hostile forces ground their arms, as for the soul of man to wait for that convenient season when the flesh will cease its solicitations, when the world will no longer seduce, and when devils shall no longer hound the pilgrim's footsteps as he treads the narrow way. As long as the soul is in the body; as long as the body inhabits the earth; and as long as the earth is accessible to the powers of hell, there will be no convenient season for man to break the bands of sin, and embrace the riches and secure the happiness which belong to followers of the Crucified. God's approval must be sought in the face of inconvenience, and won often at the cost of great tribulation.

Fifth Sunday after Trinity.

A GIRL once, sleeping in the open night, dreamed that the stars were jewels flashing from the angels' crowns. Mars burned from one angelic brow like a garnet, and Jupiter blazed from another's like a sapphire, and the clusters of Orion and Pleiades gleamed from others like the coruscations of a royal diadem. Thinking herself in heaven, she placed her hand upon her brow and found a starless crown. "Why," she cried, "does no radiant star adorn my crown?" "Because," said one who stood near her, "stars in an angel's crown represent souls rescued: you are here through God's mercy, but you have brought no one with you; therefore your crown is starless." This dream puts the most charitable and hopeful face upon inactivity. It makes it inherit a crown — though that crown was starless. The Bible makes inactivity inherit the curse of "wicked and slothful servant." There are times in men's lives when apathy is positive sin; when it is selfish to be passive, ungenerous to be inactive, soulless to be indifferent, and criminal to be neutral. Is idleness innocent when in the opening springtime the hungry earth is crying to the farmer for his seed? Is idleness innocent when in the springtime of youth, the seedtime of life, the opening heart, and plastic mind, and moulding character are crying to parent and teacher, "Now is the accepted time, now is the day of salvation"? Is inactivity ever sinless to the soul while earth's probation is the seedtime that sows for the harvest of eternity; when life is the spirit's springtime; when the real self is taking its shape and fixing its destiny for the great beyond, and when man's activities on earth shall reap the summer bloom and autumnal fruit of heaven; and his unfaithfulness shall reap the winter's blast of endless want and woe?

Is sleep safe while enemies sow tares? Is apathy harmless while thorns are growing? Is indifference innocence when pestilence is sowing its seed, or when fate "lets slip the dogs of war"? Is it less criminal while fatal error and blighting sin, while wicked men and vicious devils, are sowing thorns in the field of God and spreading pestilence

among the minds of men ; and threatening violence
to every institution which makes religion safe,
our country free, our homes happy, and our lives a
blessing?

Sixtf Sunday after Trinity.

SOME men are joyful by disposition. We like
the jovial, merry men, the Mark Tapleys of
the world, who are jolly even under adverse cir-
cumstances. Yet such joy in an irreligious man
has something sad about it. It is like building a
warm and comfortable house upon the winter's ice.
There are also men who have learned cheerfulness
because they know the wisdom and health of it.
We admire this, too — the bravery of being joyful
in this world. There is something almost tragic
in the joyous shout of the crew that goes sailing to
the polar sea. Of course they need all their hope
and cheer. Soon the sunny air will chill, the
cheerless ice will fleck the blue sea, the snow will
hiss in the brine, and the black curtain of the
Arctic night will fall over the scene. Wave your
caps, boys, as your gallant ship slips out of the
pier. Be merry if you can. I say to all, I say to
sinful men even, be cheerful if you can. But I do
not understand how it is possible to be joyous if
you look not beyond the grave into which all
things that give you joy must so soon be swept.

The joy, the merry laughter of sinful men — is it not reckless? It is like a lot of boys exhilarated by the motion of a maelstrom and shouting with delight as they are sucked into the fatal vortex. How different the Christian's joy! With God on his side, with his books balanced, with his peace sealed, with confidence in the eternal future, with the mighty conviction that all things work together for good to them that love God, — why, such a man may indulge all of the exuberance of his soul.

Seventh Sunday after Trinity.

WHISKEY! I see it first in the muck of rotting grain which the still-worm sucks with fevered breath from the sour tubs. I see it distilled drop by drop, like cold poison from the purple lips of a venomed reptile. I see it lie in darkness, gathering in its heart the fires of hell, and waiting impatient months to kindle the brain of man. I see it each black night in those dismal vaults gather within it some heart-breaking, home-blighting power. I see it sparkle in the light at last, like the changing flash of a serpent's coils or the eager glance of a hungry beast. I see it paint mirages of fountains and flowers and joy upon the brain of man, while it robs his life of its strength and his soul of its sweetness. I see it wring scalding tears from gentle eyes, and blanch and stain the cheeks of woman.   I see it steal the roses from children's faces and fill their wondering hearts with sadness. I see it cloud noble brains with suspicion and fill generous hearts with madness.   I see it quench the light from happy homes and leave them plunged in darkness through weary days of want and fear. I see it rob genius of its promise, labor of its reward, youth of its hope, and age of its repose. Language cannot paint the visions of woe which this one word waves up with its wand.   Anguish and tears and disgrace and crime and death in myriads of homes and myriads of hearts.   If there is one word that arouses all the distrust and dread and indignation of my nature, that word is whiskey!

Eighth Sunday after Trinity.

HERE is a man like a cloud, and a cloud without any silver lining.   He gets between you and the sun.   He makes everything dark. He puts the worst constructions, and attributes the worst motives, and takes the darkest view. You do not like to meet the murksome man.   You do not wish to be overcast.   Perhaps to-day you are hopeful.   You have difficulties, but by God's blessing you can work out.   Your church is struggling, but you think you see a brighter day.   You have some sorry apples in your basket, but you have gotten the big ones on top. You have a skeleton or two in your closet, but they are out of sight. The sun is shining to-day upon the high places and valleys of your landscape. And here comes that human cloud, with his shadow creeping on before him. You avoid him. You take the other side of the street. Because you know in ten minutes he would get all the small apples on the top of your basket. He would have all the skeletons out of your closet because he likes their company. You escape him, because you do not want him to cool your iron, for it is hot and you have made up your mind to strike it. Such a man may be a Christian; but he has a great besetting sin, which he must watch and pray against. Let him add this petition to his Litany: From all blue devils; from all dismal dejection; from all bilious despondency; from all funereal gloom, and from all unchristian hopelessness, — good Lord, deliver us.

Ninth Sunday after Trinity.

WHAT was the sin of Dives? It was the sin of practical unbelief. The sin of a worldly life that practically ignored God. It is the sin of the ecclesiastical Dives, the rich parish church, dwelling in the comfort and self-satisfied seclusion of congregationalism, clothed in the purple and fine linen of gorgeous architecture or art or millinery, faring sumptuously every day upon rich ritual or pulpit eloquence, and forgetting the heathen hordes, or the unreached masses which at its very gates cry for the bread of life.

Dives lifted up his eyes in hell. This vivid, pathetic, tragic picture ought to startle us into seriousness. It should thrill us with the powers of the world to come. It should keep our eyes upon eternity. It should help us to look beyond mere appearances. It should lift us above envy. It should warn us against self-centred aims. It should unmask mere conventional humanities. It should fill us with hate for the legalized luxury of Phariseeism in church and individual. It should make us take sides, at whatever cost, against the damning sin of selfish inhumanity, with which pride and fashion threaten to curse this world and make countless thousands mourn. It should inspire us to throw ourselves into the breach, and help to fill up the great gulf which yawns between men who ought to be united in the bonds of Christian fellowship, sympathy, and love.

Tenth Sunday after Trinity.

IN the palace at Versailles, as if by the irony of
fate, is a famous statue of Napoleon in exile.
His noble brow is lowered in thought, his mouth
is compressed, his chin is resting upon his breast,
and his grand eye gazes into space as if fixed on
some distant scene. There is something inexpress-
ibly sad in that strong, pale face. It is said that
the sculptor represented Napoleon at St. Helena,
just before his death. He is looking back upon
the field of Waterloo, and thinking how its fatal
issue was the result of three hours' delay. Those
three short hours seem ever to write on the walls
of his memory, — " The summer is ended, the har-
vest is past!" Years rolled on, but the memory
of that neglected opportunity follows the great
emperor through his life, and haunts him through
midnight hours in his sea-girt home. I have some-
times imagined that I could see on some remote
and lonely shore of the Lake Avernus a soul
haunted by its memories. The battle of life is
long past, centuries have rolled away, but memory
lives. Some lost soul wanders from the rest, where
the waves of that gulf beat hopelessly on the far-
off shore. The absent eye, that gazes over the
starless deep, is looking with longing unutterable
to the precious time when those who are now in

glory held up the blood-stained cross and pointed to the joys of heaven, then so near, now so far. And a bitter sigh, and a sob as bitter as despairing love, fills the solitude; but it reaches no ear, touches no sympathy, awakes no echo. Such is the vengeance of neglected opportunity.

Eleventh Sunday after Trinity.

WHEN some years ago the obstructions were blown out of "Hell-Gate," in New York harbor, it was a little child who ignited the gigantic charge. Many a night I have seen the waters whirl and seethe around those awful rocks that peeped like black demons from the foam. What fair ships were wrecked there; what treasures lost! But the days of these demons were numbered. Dynamite with its tremendous power was laid in the hewn caverns below. All was united to one electric key. The hour arrived. Who touched the key? Not the scientist's wonder-working hand; not the strong-armed man. The baby fingers of a little girl were gently laid on that key, and the work was done. The black rocks reeled back with a groan, and the waters settled down again into a smooth, safe channel, through which the white ships sail on to the depths and freedom and joy of their ocean home.

Such an electric key is the name of Jesus in the Christian's hand. Temptations may surround us upon which have wrecked our purposes and hopes. Temptations may confront us upon which thousands of souls have sunk to ruin. Devils may defy us, friends may oppose us, but Christ stands to-day the great electric key by which a child may move the omnipotent arm of God. That arm thus moved will open for us a way, safe and glorious, through the dangers of life and darkness of death, and the snares of devils, and launch us upon the boundless bosom of eternity's ocean and heaven's peace.

Twelfth Sunday after Trinity.

HOW subtle is slander! How it begins like a spark! How it glows like a cheerful fire! "Only a bit of harmless gossip." How it extends like a creeping flame! How it chars the heart! How it darkens the life like smoke!

How terrible is slander! An untimely word, an exaggeration carelessly dropped, like a coal from a woodsman's pipe, — how it spreads from tongue to tongue, from ear to ear, from house to house, with wicked haste! It hurls down characters as the fire fiend fells the trees of the forest. It crashes through family peace. It blackens names like the blackened walls of a ruin. It creates a poverty which moth and rust and thieves and fire cannot create. There is no insurance. What a great matter a little fire kindleth! A little tattle, and friends are alienated; a little gossip, and a soul is embittered; a little fun, and a good name is stabbed. A little spite, and a legion of devils are aroused, — devils of suspicion and doubt and hate, that can never be allayed. A handful of seed sown in the night, and to-morrow the tares and the thorns are growing in the Kingdom, to bear their perpetual, never-ending harvest of tears and blood.

Thirteenth Sunday after Trinity.

IN church work it is generally the case that those who do the least work do the most complaining. You hear them say, "The church is in a bad way, the people are unsocial, the mission work is feeble, the singing is not congregational, the services are cold, the finances are unsatisfactory." Even if these things are true, no church member has a right to say so until he has won the right by doing everything in his power to remedy them. All this reminds me of a little incident of my college days. Henry Brown went away, and asked Barnwell to take care of some pots of flowers in his room. In a few days Barnwell wrote Brown a postal card, "Dear Brown, your flowers are all dying; I think it is for lack of water." Now, I say, if the Church of God needs watering, in the name of God, men and women, go and water it. If the church is unsocial, do your part to make it social. If it needs mission work, stop talking and go to work. If the responses are cold, lift your voices to make them warm. Join in the singing; deny yourself to swell the finances. Take a hand yourself where help is needed. If every faultfinder and drone in the Kingdom would say, " This is largely my fault," and then arouse himself to build before his own door, the scene would remind one of the resurrection which Ezekiel saw in the valley of dry bones.

Fourteenth Sunday after Trinity.

THAT which in the darkness seems but one talent of silver may in the light prove to be a talent of gold. A woman in Lincolnshire thought it a small thing that she was teaching a dull little boy his figures; but that boy was Isaac Newton, and those figures reached the stars. The obscure teacher at Eisleben esteemed very lightly, no doubt, his school of peasant boys, but among them was one who should shake off the shackles of Europe. The names of the men are forgotten who taught Shakespeare to write, who gave Rubinstein his first music lesson, who showed Titian how to mix colors, who gave Christopher Wren his first lesson in architecture.   Those men built wiser than they knew who brought John Wesley and Francis Xavier and Hugh Latimer to Christ.   It is thrilling to think of the Sunday-school classes where there were boys who answered, when the roll was called, to the names of William Muhlenburg, Charles Spurgeon, William Gladstone, Henry Liddon, Frederick Farrar, James Garfield, James McCosh.

Schiller, in his Song of the Bell, makes the master of the foundry encourage an exhausted moulder in the ditch by telling him that the work which he is doing in that dark ditch will one day speak from the eminence of towers, with tongues of eloquence and melody to thronging multitudes. Who can tell?   Perhaps the influence of the humble home shall one day speak from the eminence of a noble life, with the eloquence of a Christian character and the melody of a pious spirit.   Perhaps the lessons of the Sunday-school will speak from the pulpit with the eloquence of truth, or from the altar with the melody of devotion.   Perhaps the work of the quiet day school will speak in senate halls with a statesman's wisdom and a patriot's eloquence.   Yes, and the work of the humble Christian shall be blessed.   It may be done in the darkness of obscurity or suffering, but

it will speak like Schiller's bells from the eminence
of heaven's towers, sending out their voices of
praise and music and joy to swell the hallelujah
chorus of harpers' harps and seraphs' songs.

Fifteenth Sunday after Trinity.

BY the beautiful parable of the Good Samaritan
it was not Christ's purpose to cast any re-
flection upon the ecclesiastical orders of his day.
Nor did he intend to approve of the doctrines of
the Samaritans. But by the heartless neglect of
men of holy profession on the one hand, and by
the simple charity of the heretic on the other, he
desired to exalt the beauty and grace of charity,
by showing us that its absence robs the holiest
office of its sanctity, and that its presence covers
the multitude of sins. Without charity the priest's
pure robes are slurred with ignominy, and with it
Jim Bludso's charred and rugged form is glorified
by a halo of light. The parable of the Good
Samaritan is intended to rebuke mere theoretical
religion, which contents itself with paper schemes
for the reduction of poverty or the relief of dis-
tress. It rebukes the formalist's religion, which is
satisfied with the punctilious performance of out-
side show and ritual observance. It rebukes
ascetic religion, that one-eyed piety which sees

only God and forgets man. Theories and forms are most valuable if they are means to an end. If not, they are child's toys in men's hands. The value of theories and rituals and forms is as scaffolding upon which to build holy lives and practical beneficence.

Sixteenth Sunday after Trinity.

THE great mass of men believe in papal infallibility, but they do not place the triple crown on the head of Leo XIII. They place it, each one on his own head. Of course, there are different degrees of loyalty to this infallible I, but few are altogether free from it. It is hard for a man to dispossess himself of the idea that he is the centre of the universe, and that things are far and near as they are far and near to him. Thus things are important as they are important to him. The far-off star seems smaller than the neighboring moon. The billions of people in a remote planet are of less consequence than the few people in my village. The shipwreck of a thousand Chinese is of less consequence than a case of diphtheria in my family. Thus man considers himself the centre of all things, and he measures out from himself. He is the starting-point and the standard of measurement. This natural tendency, if permitted to grow, will extend not only to physical, but to social and moral things. Soon he will measure men and creeds and truth, and even God himself, by his own stature. Thus men will be good if they are good to him. They are wise if they agree with him. They are on the right side if they are on his side. And even God is near or far, good or cruel, as the ways of Providence meet with his approval or inclinations. When one has gotten to that point, and many have, he has gotten to such contraction and narrow-mindedness that, in comparison with it, the most sectarian bigotry would be delightful liberality.

Seventeenth Sunday after Trinity.

HERE is a large vineyard. Many men and maidens are busy on the hillside. They are coming and going, and singing the vintage songs. Here is the master. He sees that the rules are kept. There must be no disorder, no profanity. Each must keep his place. The baskets must be clean. The master is counting the baskets that are brought to the vats. After each name he writes the number of baskets brought. At last the week is ended, and the men and maidens come to receive their pay. Here among them is a man whom the master has been watching day by day. He kept his basket clean; he kept his place; he used no profane language; he enjoyed the companionship of the others; he joined merrily in the vintage songs. But in all this time he gathered no grapes.

"What is your name?" says the master.

"Menalque," says the man.

"I find your name upon the book," replies the master, "but I do not find that you gathered a single cluster; there is, therefore, no pay for you."

"No pay?" says the man. "What have I done wrong? I have kept my place, used no improper language, kept my basket clean, and joined heartily in the songs."

"You did no wrong," says the master, "but you did no work. There is nothing for you."

"No pay for me!" exclaimed the man. "Why, that is the one thing I came in the vineyard for. The pay constituted my chief interest in it."

Is not this the history of thousands in the Lord's vineyard? They come, their names are upon the book. They do no special wrong; they do not swear, or steal, or commit adultery. They break no rule. They sing the vintage songs. They hear sermons, if they are entertaining. They attend church, if it is quite convenient. But are they in any true sense laborers in God's vineyard? Have they done any honest work for Christ and his church? Have they performed one hard task, done one unpleasant duty, spoken one brave word, lifted one fallen sinner, lightened one heavy burden, crucified one loved comfort, or done any one thing or series of things that would justly entitle them to the name of laborer, or the hope of reward when the great day of reckoning comes?

Eighteenth Sunday after Trinity.

THE most remarkable figure in human history is the Carpenter of Nazareth, standing among the shavings of his humble shop, in an isolated village, and saying without passion or enthusiasm, " Heaven and earth shall pass away, but my words shall not pass away."

With no agencies with which to accomplish his designs, he announces that He is a king, and that his kingdom shall have no end. This penniless, powerless, almost friendless Man declares that this kingdom shall be co-extensive with the earth as well as with time. His followers shall be, not individuals, but nations. "Go!" He says to men equally provincial and obscure and poor. " Go into all the world, and make disciples of all nations." He admits that his principles will not be popular, that his laws shall antagonize what men love, and oppose their selfish instincts ; but He calmly foretells the time when his cause shall triumph, and when He, the Nazarene, and the hungry, homeless peasant, shall become the centre of the world's thought, and the object of its affection.

We have become so accustomed to all this that we forget how wonderful it is. We forget the poverty and obscurity of this Carpenter. We forget the extent of his conquests and his influence. The proud nineteenth century, progressive America and rich Europe, must concede that this provincial Jew is influencing the world to-day from end to end ; and that, with all the world's advancement in learning, enlightenment, invention, and science, his name is a living power compared with which the names of boasted moderns and the names of all earth's great ones are but the favorite playthings of an age. Whatever might have been the case had we lived in the days of Peter and Nicodemus and Caiaphas, we are now no longer ashamed to call the Nazarene our King. The carpenter's coat can no longer hide his divinity.

Nineteenth Sunday after Trinity.

FREDERICK THE GREAT'S biographer considers one of his best claims to that title was his courage to say in a military despatch, " We have lost a great battle, and it is all my fault." It takes greatness of mind and nobility of heart to confess personal blame for real disaster, when the blame might be thrown on others. It takes a generous heart to be a just judge when our own interests are at the bar, or to concede the fairness of the decision which presses the laurel crown upon another's brow instead of mine; to believe in the justice of the world when it fails to appreciate what we think ourselves to be, and to approve its good sense when we are not taken into the lap of its favor. It takes a great mind and a broad mind to look first to its own life for the cause of failure, before it looks to the fault of others. It takes a brave and a wise heart to realize that behind the clouds the sun is still shining; that the world moves on after age has blinded my eyes so that I cannot see its progress; that God is good in the midst of personal disaster, and wise when my favorite purposes are thwarted; and to cry out in times of darkness and doubt, "I must decrease; but Christ, and right, and goodness, and justice, and love must increase more and more, until the perfect day."

Twentieth Sunday after Trinity.

THE universal brotherhood of man is a new and original doctrine of Christ. The nearest approach to it that I have been able to find in the classics is where Plato says, "All of you in the state are undoubtedly brethren." But even here he confines the brotherhood to the state. To the Greek, outsiders were barbarians. To the Jew, outsiders were Gentiles. With Christ there were no outsiders. There were no conventional barriers, no race obstructions, no color line, no ecclesiastical fence, no sectarian hedge, no national wall, no ocean's breadth that could confine his love or circumscribe his sympathy. Man is my brother. What a splendid conception of man! What a blessing to learn this of Christ, and to feel our own souls grow and broaden under its influence! How it sweeps the cobwebs from the brain; how it throws open the windows of the heart, letting the light in, dispelling the close, foul odors of selfishness, frightening the skeletons from narrow closets, and illuminating the dark corners of private grief, to feel that

" A man's a man for a' that!"

How the power and beauty of this Christian humanity lifts us above and bears us over all distance and all time, over continent's stretch and ocean's storm, over race prejudice and sectarian bigotry and political passion, and social caste and selfish love!

Twenty-first Sunday after Trinity.

SOME of our stiff-starched, highly moral infidels have made a great discovery. They have found some unclean animals in the ark. They have discovered some goats in the sheep pasture. They arch their sanctimonious eyebrows and talk about the hypocrites in the church. The truth is, there are no greater hypocrites on earth than these fellows who think they are so good that they need neither God nor Saviour. But what of this discovery, so startling, so damaging? What of these hypocrites in the church? Is the charge true? It is, if the Bible is true. These astounding exposures of the church's delinquencies, pointed out with ill-concealed pleasure by unbelieving Pharisees, were foretold by Jesus, and nailed as a devil's trick, more than eighteen centuries ago. The parable of the tares is devoted to this very subject. When the tares, which at first are beautiful, begin to bear fruit, heresy, worldliness, intemperance, fraud, right in the heart of the holy church, the community is shocked, the tattling wires whisper. The very sensation made is a tribute to the church. Satan's friends rejoice. The ethical, æsthetical, agnostical Pharisee draws his skirts about him. The servants of God are made sick at heart. Disappointed, frightened, mortified, they are driven to their Master, and cry, "Sir, didst thou not sow good seed in thy field? From whence, then, hath it tares?" Christ says it is the devil. "An enemy hath done this." Not God's decree, not the church's fault, but the devil. Christ exonerates his servants and puts this thing where it belongs. It is a campaign trick. It is wonderful how men have been caught by this shallow device; especially when the trap was so explicitly pointed out by our Lord.

The church is no more unworthy because of its hypocrites than money is valueless because of counterfeits, than the legal profession is worthless because of its pettifoggers, than the medical profession is useless because of its quacks, than trade is untrustworthy because of its fraudulent bankrupts.

Twenty-second Sunday after Trinity.

ONE charm of biography is its exhibition of great men's inner lives. It shows us the human heart behind the scenes of public life and genius. This is the charm of the Gospel. This is the power of Christianity. We no longer follow a metaphysical deity hidden in effulgence. God is not presented as a conception, but as a life — a life from the womb to the tomb. This life gives concrete form to divine attributes. After I have

seen Niagara I have a new thought of grandeur.
After I know Jesus I have a new thought of good-
ness and compassion. " The light of the knowl-
edge of the glory of God is in the face of Jesus
Christ." Here is the value of the incarnation.
Here is its necessity. Of course, this coalition of
deity and humanity is wonderful and inexplicable.
But it is not more wonderful nor more incredible
than the mysterious union of soul and body.
Emmanuel, God with us, is Christ's conquering
name. It is the man-God that has conquered the
world, and overcome its doubts and pride and
swords. It is the God-man that is the central
truth of the Gospel, and the highest manifestation
of the love and condescension of God.

Twenty-third Sunday after Trinity.

HIGH among the Alps, at the foot of the great
Rhone glacier, there flows forth a bold
stream from the moraine of boulders and sand and
broken ice. This is the beginning of the River
Rhone. It then looks like a stream of dirty milk.
I followed this boiling, turbid torrent a hundred
miles. With frantic fury it plunges along its
course, bearing its burden of dirt —always discol-
ored, always vehement, whether thundering over
the boulders, or crashing down amidst the Alpine

pines, or sweeping through the grassy meadows of the high Swiss valley, or hastening past the houses of Martigny or St. Maurice. At last a little less boisterous, but still impure and discolored, it discharges itself into Lake Geneva. At the other end of this crescent lake the river resumes its career to the sea. It is a beautiful lake, indeed, that the Rhone has rested in; so serene, so translucent, so deep, so blue! So picturesque with its vine-clad hills, and its nestling villages, and its blue peaks and its distant glimpses of the snow crown of Mont Blanc! So historic with its Chillon, and its Vevey, and its Lausanne! And here is Geneva, with its John Calvin's church and its Rousseau's island and its bridges. Here the Rhone resumes its course to the sea. Let us stand here on this bridge, and watch the river flow out of the lake. How swift and strong it glides by the stone arches! Still full of spirit and energy and life, but clear as crystal. No gritty foam, no grimy impurity, no burden of mud and sand. In its rapid and transparent depths every brown pebble and every white shell shines upon the bottom. Beautiful river! pure, unsullied, sparkling, powerful, rejoicing, crystalline!

Now, then, what Lake Geneva is to the Rhone, religion should be to man. Man, with feverish heart, with tumultuous thoughts and doubts, with terrible temptations, with soiled soul and turbid life, with wild upliftings of hope and black chasms of despair! Let the Gospel be your Lake Geneva. The Gospel with its tranquil depths, with its sunny hopes, with its mirrored mountain tops, and skies of eternal blue! Let your turbulent soul rest in the Gospel and then go on its strong way rejoicing, — its forces not abated, but chastened; no part of your life destroyed, but all of it consecrated, all of it purified, all of it turned into one pure, strong stream of manly devotion to truth, righteousness, and God. Then will your life be like the River Rhone below the lake, where it marks a broad belt of fertility, prosperity, and peace through the fair fields of France; until it is lost at last in the purple waters of the south, where ceaseless summer smiles upon the leaping, laughing waves of the jubilant sea.

Twenty-fourth Sunday after Trinity.

THERE are about eight millions of sermons preached in the United States every year. One would imagine that the whole land would bow before such an effort. It reminds me of the first battle I ever saw. I was a boy and only a spectator. I thought everybody would be killed. There were such thousands of guns fired, such clouds of smoke and dust, such frightful noise and

yells. But when it was all over only one man was
dead and a dozen wounded. So on Sunday night,
when the last reverberation of the pulpit has died
out, what multitudes remain as they were before.
Now this is a great evil, this hearing of sermons,
prayers, and hymns. with unmoved hearts and un-
moved wills. The services become a mere perform-
ance, an attraction. an entertainment. The congre-
gation becomes an audience. The people are critics
instead of participants. The liar praises a sermon
on lying; the slanderer is amused at the good hits
on slander. A faithful sermon on sin is preached,
and the sinners go chatting gayly home, discussing
the preacher's theology, his rhetoric, his delivery;
anything but the question, " What must I do to be
saved?" We have a thousand men interested in
theology where there is one interested in personal
religion. Vast numbers discuss theoretical re-
ligion, many discuss it well. They are walking
concordances.

> " In religion,
> What damned error, but some sober brow
> Will bless it, and approve it with a text?"

Zealous for the progress of some ecclesiastical or-
ganization, bigoted in some dogmatic system, they
care little for their own souls and sins, or for the
nourishment of their own piety. No doubt, it was
to such as these that the Lord alluded when he
closed the Sermon upon the Mount. Their mag-

nificent superstructure of ecclesiasticism will be found to be built upon the sand, and will fall with terrible ruin in that day and hour when real and vital religion is needed.

Twenty-fifth Sunday after Trinity.

MANY years ago my esteemed friend Col. Boyd of Wytheville, Virginia, gave to a Frenchman, by the name of Hartmann, a rocky hillside. Everywhere the hard, blue limestone protruded. A more unpromising garden could not be imagined. In the spring the warmth and moisture made the hillside green for a little while, but the first drought scorched it dry and brown. But Hartmann worked away, patiently, perseveringly, systematically. He dug out the rocks, he deepened the soil, he irrigated from the neighboring brook. Years passed, and the " Frenchman's Garden," as everybody called it, was the most beautiful, the most picturesque, the most fruitful, the most profitable garden in all of that part of Virginia. So, after all, that peculiar kind of human hearts which the Lord described as " stony places " are not absolutely hopeless. These shallow hearts may be deepened. This sentimental religion may be enriched. The Word of God may be cultivated until it grows to be a fruitful plant in even these unpromising lives. From being a mere enthusiasm, or a dead orthodoxy, religion may become a life, a deep-rooted life, a life hid with Christ in God.

St. Andrew's Day.

ANDREW was a quiet man, overshadowed by his bold and boisterous brother Simon. Yet it was his quiet influence that brought that impetuous fisherman to the Lord. His devout life found Jesus first. Then he did that quiet and beautiful thing of carrying his religion to his own home. As soon as he was convinced that Jesus was the Messiah, Andrew "findeth his own brother Simon." This is all the more beautiful because it is so uncommon. How very rare it is that a man is a missionary in his own household! Is it because the people know him too well? A man is ashamed to preach to those who have seen him lose his temper over a badly cooked breakfast. A woman hesitates to talk of heaven to those who know how devoted she is to earth. Yet St. Andrew, with his quiet reality, with his unpretentious genuineness, went home and carried the good news to those nearest and dearest to him. And such was his character that they believed him. Simon did not doubt his brother's judgment. He went with him at once to Jesus. The first man ever brought to Christ, and Andrew brought him. Immediately the more brilliant, the more impetuous, the more daring brother goes to the front of the sacred narrative. And Andrew continued his work unheralded and unsung, until on the lonely Euxine shores he won the martyr's crown on St. Andrew's cross. He was no meteor flashing through the historic sky, but a well-trimmed lamp. Who can tell, but God, the influence and good, the glory and peace, of this faithful, humble life?

St. Thomas's Day.

DO not exercise your doubts. Exercise your faith. Doubt is weakness, faith is power; doubt is disease, faith is health. Let the sick part rest. Exercise the well part, and it will encroach more and more until it drives out the sickness. Take care of your faith, however small, as the famine-stricken guard the scanty seed grain, as the snow-bound, lost woodsman nurses his last match. Little faith may grow to great faith and become a power. "What a great matter a little fire kindleth." Do not think about your doubts. Intellectualize your faith, exercise it, use your ingenuity upon it, see what can be done with it, live up to it, what there is of it. Yonder at Niagara you see the graceful steel bridge span the chasm where the untamed whirlpool thunders below. How leapt that span from cliff to cliff? They say a tiny kite flew over the chasm and fell upon the other side. The chasm was spanned. You say by a thread. Yes, by a thread. But the thread was used to pull over a cord, and the cord to pull over a rope, and the rope a chain, and the chain a cable, and on the cable was built the bridge, upon whose strong and steadfast span the massive trains crash across. Thus may it be with the most attenuated thread of faith. What possibilities, what destinies, hang upon it! Ah! it may be lightly snapped asunder. But that thread may grow to a cord, and the cord to a rope, and the rope to a cable, and the cable to a bridge, spanning the chasm between heaven and earth. And our prayers shall ascend, and God's blessings shall descend, like the angels ascending and descending on the ladder which Jacob saw.

St. Stephen's Day.

THE first martyr, St. Stephen, being dead, yet speaketh. Martyrdom is one of the original ideas of Christianity. Martyrdom means that Truth is inviolable. Truth must be inviolate if we have to die for it. The particular truth for which St. Stephen died was that God's love is not pent up in Jewish rituals and Jewish creeds ;

" That the love of God is broader
    Than the measure of man's mind ;
And the heart of the Eternal
    Is most wonderfully kind."

Those who claimed a monopoly of God's favor became infuriated that a mere youth should preach forcibly, irresistibly, that their boasted monopoly was an imposture. So they killed him, — this youth, full of faith and of the Holy Ghost. He breathed his brave soul out in a prayer to Jesus. Ah, here was a fragrant, holy life, rebuking with its earnest spirit the careless and the aimless ; rebuking with its brief career those who excuse their fruitless life by lack of time ; rebuking with its humble station those who excuse their idleness by want of influence. Look you upon this picture, this mere deacon, this martyred youth, with his angel's face glowing in the focus of God's smile, standing out effulgent against the shadowed background of hate.

St. John the Evangelist's Day.

WEARY years after the other apostles had died, years after Jerusalem had fallen, thirty years after St. Peter and St. Paul had suffered martyrdom, sixty years — which is a long,

long time — after the crucifixion, St. John the
Divine still lived.   He was a very, very aged man.
Yet his unfailing faculties were to the last the
chosen channels of Revelation.   What a retrospect
had been his !   What religious and civil revolu-
tions had swept the earth in his time !   What
strong men had he seen bowed down !   What
sowers to the flesh had he seen reap corruption !
What proud hearts had he seen humbled !   Oh,
the fair forms and the beautiful faces ! — he had
seen them wither.   How had he seen the mighty
fallen !   Eleven Roman emperors had risen from
the horizon of obscurity, had blazed in their merid-
ian splendor.   St. John had seen them sink, one
after another, quenched in a sea of blood.   Won-
derful had been his worldly experience ; but more
wonderful his heavenly vision.   All earthly things
were like the fragments of sea-weeds and the
broken spars of noble ships and the brave men's
bleaching bones that lay scattered along Patmos's
storm-beat strand ; and spiritual things were like
the calm heavens above and the stars that roll for-
ever on — so great, so high, so unmoved by earth's
far-off storms and petty strifes, that seem so great
to us.

Conversion of St. Paul.

THERE is one figure in history which all criti-
cism cannot efface; it is Paul at Damascus.
I have often thought of those three days and
nights, through whose weary, silent hours he sat
sightless, foodless, motionless, in that house in
the street called "Straight." What a time for
reflection! What a time to detect imposture,
if there should be any! What a time to
dispel illusions! What a time, too, to review
the recent scenes at Jerusalem! Paul was well
equipped for this investigation. He was an eye-
witness. He knew the men who had crucified
Jesus. He had talked with the men who claimed
to have seen him arisen. He was thoroughly famil-
iar with the case. He had, moreover, a well-
trained mind — logical, clear, and pains-taking.
He was not willing to give up without a terrible
struggle. The old faith died hard. The new
faith antagonized all his instincts and interests.
It was an obscure and despised religion. Paul
was not dazzled by the glamour of a victorious
Church. His pride was at stake. He had been
aggressive in his opposition to that which he was
now called upon to espouse. He must resign
country, social position, and friends. The Lord
promised him this: "I will show him how great

things he must suffer for my name's sake." In undisturbed silence he went over the evidence and came to his conclusion. After three days and nights he came out from the purgatorial fires of suspense and conflict. He came with a decision with which he was willing to face any criticism; for which he was willing to endure any hardship, live any life, and die any death. How irresistible is such a decision, from such a man, and under such circumstances!

The Purification.

WHAT a scene for painters, what a theme for poets, what a text for preachers, is the Purification of the Virgin! There is the aged Simeon, who, like the old covenant, could not die till he had seen the Lord; singing his Nunc Dimittis, that dying-swan note of Old Testament psalmody. There was the holy Anna, a widow indeed, the first of that countless throng of faithful women who should proclaim the Christ. There was the blessed Mary, who came in her pious poverty to offer her doves in the temple, and in reality offered the Lamb of God. There was the Holy Child, a helpless babe, symbol of the coming "New," as Simeon and Anna were types of the going "Old." Rubens and Guido Reni, Paul

Veronese and Titian, Raphael and Rembrandt, have drawn inspiration from these holy scenes and left in living colors their thoughts about them. May they also inspire us to living deeds! May the Holy Spirit lead us to the Temple of God; may we meet the Lord there. May it be our day of purification. May we all at last with Simeon sing, " Now, Lord, lettest thou thy servant depart in peace, for mine eyes have seen thy salvation."

St. Matthias's Day.

THE most that we know of this apostle is that he took the place of one who failed in life's mission. Matthias was the successor of Judas. Man is honored — Paul and Judas, you and I, are honored with a place in the great plan of God. If we are faithful, our names are wrought into the eternal fabric. If we are faithless, God does his work with other agents. He can raise up the stones into Abraham's seed. He can make the stones cry out, if men are dumb. The work goes on ; it does not cease when our connection with it ceases. Other names take the place on the roll of God's co-workers where our names were blotted out. He calls us to labor in the vineyard, not because he needs workers, but because we need work. Ourselves are the greatest losers by our failure, the greatest gainers by our fidelity.

The Annunciation.

WHILE Gabriel winged his strong flight from heaven to earth, many a Jewish woman's heart fluttered with the hope that the Messiah would be born of her. Many a proud mansion would have welcomed Heaven's herald then. There were gorgeous palaces in the world, in those days, that could have received even an angel with sumptuous honors. There was the magnificence of Herod the Great, and the splendor of Augustus. But "God hath chosen the weak things of the world to confound the things that are mighty." Past Rome's grandeur and Jerusalem's pride, the angel swept on to the nestling mountain hamlet, to the humble home, to the blessed Virgin, and there announced God's gift to Mary, to Israel, and to mankind. With all the help of beautiful legends and the inspiration of Italy's art we still fall short in fancy of the greatness and beauty of this scene — this angel's visit to this handmaid of the Lord, Heaven's chosen instrument of the Holy Ghost.

I think all Christians may join in the angel's salutation, and heartily say at least this much of the Ave Maria, — " Hail, Mary, full of grace, the Lord is with thee. Blessed art thou among women, and blessed is the fruit of thy womb!"

St. Mark's Day.

IT is an interesting thing to watch an ocean ship get out from London docks. How helpless she is! She cannot use her machinery. Her sails are furled. She is pushed forward and backward. She is pulled along by puffing tugs. She stops to let other vessels pass. She waits through weary hours. She moves on again. But she is hindered and limited and retarded. But some progress is rewarding her perseverance. She is getting more room. She begins to ply her engines. But she must go slowly. She must be cautious. Then there is more liberty; there are fewer obstructions and fewer conditions. The river is wider. The city is being left behind, with its din and its sin. The fresh air revives the sailor. He unfurls his canvas. He moves steadily on to the line where river fades into sea. He hears the music of the surf beating upon the sand. He sees the white-caps marching across the blue prairies of ocean. And at last the gallant ship, emancipated, seems to stretch herself, and expand herself, and swell and sway and bow in ecstasy, as she speeds her way over the billowy fields of her native heath and boundless home. Thus it is with the soul that is escaping from the trammels of the flesh, and the limitations and the conditions imposed upon it by

the world. How slow its progress is at first! How
it is pushed forward and falls backward! How
crippled is the soul's splendid machinery! how
awkward its movements! Its sails are furled. It
must submit to be helped by things smaller than
itself — by trivial rules and puerile helps. It
stops. It waits. It stands to for obstructions.
But it moves on. It makes a little progress. The
channel is getting wider. The shores of earth are
getting further away. There is more room, more
freedom. The engines move. The sails are
thrown out. The fresh air of grace gladdens the
sailor, and tells him that the city of sin is fading
in the distance. The ocean of liberty is reached at
last. The Lord takes the helm. The Spirit of
God fills the sails, and then, emancipated and free,
unloosed from the devil's imprisonment, unshackled
from the habits and slavery of flesh, unlimited and
unconditioned by the world's conventionalities, the
glad soul rejoices on the bosom of God, which is
the soul's ocean, which is the soul's home.

Sts. Philip and James's Day.

IF a man has sinned, he has sinned. It is done.
And nothing can make the fact not a fact.
The sin has been committed. It has gone upon
record. It has become forever a part of the man's
history. It is woven into the very warp of his

past. The materialist's mud can hide it only for a time. The flowers of the infidel's rhetoric can cover it but for the moment. Beneath flowers and mud, the sin is still engraved on the very adamant of fact. Macbeth may incarnadine the multitudinous seas, his royal spouse may use all the perfumes of Arabia; but the fact remains indelible, imperishable. The promise of future good behavior may bless the future, but it cannot make the past not to have been. Recent discoveries have revealed the carcasses of prehistoric animals thrown out at the foot of a Siberian glacier. These animals were preserved unchanged, unseen, and unknown, for untold centuries, beneath the frozen mud and the solid ice of the never-hasting, never-resting, ever-moving glacier. And when, at last, these long-preserved carcasses came out to the light and warmth and sun, they sent forth their horrid stench. Thus sin may be buried under the mud of materialism, and be frozen in indifference and hidden in oblivion for years and centuries and cycles, but the on-moving glacier of time will at last reveal them to the light and glory of the Judgment Day, and then will they stink in the nostrils of God, and of angels, and of all the assembled multitudes.

St. Barnabas's Day.

I HAVE no doubt that Barnabas stood very high — even among the very highest of those men who won the world for Christ in the apostolic times. As a living power, as an active factor, he is much more prominent than most of the apostles, and is inferior only to St. Peter and St. Paul. The very title that the disciples gave him, " Barnabas," or " Son of Consolation," shows what he was to them. With a personal presence which made the Greeks at Lystra take him for Jupiter, with a liberality which laid his fortune at the apostles' feet, with the scriptural knowledge which belongs to a Levite, with broad sympathies and fervid eloquence, he must, indeed, have been a great consolation to that feeble and struggling band, which had just faced the appalling task of evangelizing a world. Even after eighteen centuries of work, after so much has been done, we feel that it would still be a great consolation if young men of wealth and beauty and learning and eloquence would give themselves, as Barnabas did, to the ministry of Christ, and the promotion of that one cause which is most worthy of noble gifts and exalted talents.

The Nativity of St. John the Baptist.

WE have seen on some beautiful morning the sun rising in glory out of the east, and the moon still fair and bright in the west. This is what I think of when I think of Jesus and St. John the Baptist. The rising sun, the setting moon. One increaseth, the other decreaseth. Not because they antagonize each other, but because the inferior fades before the superior splendor. One closes the dispensation to which it belongs — the night. The other opens the dispensation which belongs to it — the day. One has the beauty of a recluse ; the other comes to mingle with the activities and sorrows and joys of men. One gives borrowed light; the other is light in its essence. One gives light that is transient; the other stores light and heat in everything that it touches. The one is negative — preaching repentance ; the other is constructive and productive — founding a kingdom.

John the Baptist, as we look back at him, seems greater than any other prophetic star that shines in the welkin of the Jewish Church. Not that he is really greater by material measurement; but because he reflects more than any other prophet the glory of the Sun of Righteousness.

St. Peter's Day.

WHAT very human stuff the apostles were
made of! Take Simon Peter, for instance.
It is very instructive, almost amusing, to think
that a great ecclesiastic should have been made
out of him. A young fisherman, with a powerful
physique, a brawny arm, an impetuous temper,
a generous heart, a vigorous mind, an elementary
education, a good trade, an humble home, and a
young wife. That was the raw material of him!
Would it not be well if people bore in mind the
raw material of the clergy? A gentleman com-
plaining of the clergy received the apology that
they were made out of the laity. Ministers may
say, with Shylock: "Have we not eyes? Have we
not hands, organs, dimensions, passions? Fed by
the same food, hurt by the same weapons, subject
to the same diseases, healed by the same means,
warmed and cooled by the same winter and summer
that you are? If you prick us will we not bleed?
If you tickle us will we not laugh? If you poison
us will we not die?" If this were remembered,
perhaps ministers would frequently get forbearance
instead of criticism, prayers instead of blame, sym-
pathy instead of prejudice, and help instead of hurt
feelings and injured innocence.

The Apostle St. James's Day.

THE headless body of St. James lay upon the
bloody sand. Thus drank this "son of
thunder" of the cup that his Lord had drunk
before; thus was he baptized with his Master's
baptism. And Herod, his murderer, looked with
satisfied pride and brutal scorn upon the mangled
corpse. And Herod, arrayed in a robe of shim-
mering gold, was hailed as a god. Here are
apparent success and failure side by side. Wher-
upon I will take up my parable:

One hot August morning in 1884, I stood and
gazed at the graceful form of Vesuvius as it lifted
its proud head into the blue sky. I traversed the
city and began the circuitous ascent. And at last,
after hours of weary toil, I reached the top. I
stood upon the rough, ashy rim of the crater.
Around me is a circle of cinders and stones and
sulphur. Below me is a lake burning with fire
and brimstone — a turbulent lake, angry and fu-
rious, sinking and swelling, hissing and boiling
and seething; receding to awful depths and rising
almost to my feet! Blue blazes creep over the
surface like serpents, and red flames leap up from
the abyss. White jets of steam hiss high in air,
and black clouds of smoke roll over the valley.
The noise grows louder, the heat more intense,

the stench more unendurable, and at last an explo-
sion of fearful force throws me almost from my
feet, and I turn and flee in terror. And as I flee
down the ashy cone I see the valley which I have
left that morning. I see the winding road playing
hide and seek among the olives and the vines.
I see the white villas, more and more numerous till
the city is reached. I see Naples like a crescent
encircling the sea. Its domes and spires gleam in
the light. I see the beautiful bay with its dotted
sails of many a hue. I see the blue mountains in
the distance. I see the broad Mediterranean, with
its isles. In that atmosphere the horizon is clearly
lined. No veil of mist intercepts the gladdened
gaze while the Italian sky bends down to kiss the
dimpled sea.

All of this I left behind as I climbed the rugged
heights to a lake of fire. So had Herod, and so
has many a man, when he thought he had reached
the summit of human glory, reached the brink of
hell. And as he turns in terror from the unveiled
fury, he sees — alas, too late! — what he has left be-
hind him. He has been climbing away with weary
steps from Paradise — away from the city that
hath foundations. away from the sea of glass, which
the prophet saw in heaven as the symbol of eternal
peace.

The Transfiguration.

O N Hermon's heaven-kissing summit, encircled by gleaming snow, under stars that burned bright through the high crystal air, had climbed a little company of men. Jesus and Peter and James and John. Jesus and the three disciples who had seen Jairus's daughter raised, the same three who should see Gethsemane's bloody sweat. Jesus prayed, and as he prayed, the veil of human flesh could no longer conceal his inner radiance. A halo of glory enveloped Him, and his person shone with an effulgence that put to shame the pearly snows of Hermon. And his celestial splendor drew the very spirits from their concealment, and gave them palpable form. Moses, the greatest man who had yet walked the earth, and Elijah, the greatest prophet, stood before the carnal eyes of mortal men. They talked with Jesus on the highest theme that thought can touch — his death. And here, on this mountain top, away from human strife and joy, while the busy world was hushed in sleep, chosen men were made the eye-witnesses of the majesty of Christ. And here was manifested with startling realism the communion of saints in heaven and earth; the union of the church militant and the church triumphant; the continuous life of the old covenant with the new; the recog-

nition of departed saints; and the Kingship of
Christ over both the quick and dead.   How
calm was the carpenter's Son amidst these super-
natural scenes which overwhelmed with wonder
and fear the other men ! Yet the frightened
Simon felt that he would perpetuate this splendor
and detain this holy company. But that could
not be yet. It must be reached by cross-bearing
for Simon and for Jesus too. And the memory of
this scene would sustain them all. It would
strengthen Jesus in Gethsemane and on Calvary.
It would sustain these disciples through their
faithful lives and martyr's death.

St. Bartholomew's Day.

WE know next to nothing about this man
Bartholomew. He was no genius ; he made
no stir. He did not come to prominence either as
a Simon Peter or a Judas Iscariot. He was one
of the obscure, unknown Christians. Yet these
men make up the army of God. It is the aggre-
gate of small things that make life. It is the
stream of pennies that fill the treasury of God.
The numberless leaves make the forest; the in-
numerable sands bound the sea. Not brilliant
efforts, but repeated efforts, carry on the world's
progress. Thread by thread the cloth is woven;

rail by rail the bands of steel encircle the earth; brick by brick the city is built. The one-talented men, like Bartholomew, make the world and the church. The important people are the privates rather than the generals, the machinists rather than the mechanics, the ploughmen rather than the agriculturists, the pioneers rather than the emigrant agents, the loomsmen rather than the overseers, the faithful men of mediocrity rather than the brilliant men of genius.

St. Matthew's Day.

ST. MATTHEW, the publican, the business man, the householder, was called away from the receipt of custom to serve Christ. He was well-to-do, but served God. One of the greatest and perhaps the latest triumphs of Christianity will be the consecration of wealth and the power of wealth. Riches are intrinsically noble ; they have power to create much noble beauty and joy. But they have been in the hands of the devil. They have been used to debase and harden and corrupt men. They have made men forget God. Trusting in riches and love of money has imperilled millions of souls. Many a man has lost his innocence through haste to be rich. Heaping up money has debased many a character. How great

then, because how rare, to wrest the power from
evil, to make money a blessing, to use it as a
stewardship from God, and to bestow it liberally
as gifts, instead of having it wrung from us as
spoils.

St. Michael's and All Angels' Day.

ANGELS' visits, few and far between, are
always ushered in with suitable conditions.
No common scenes invite them, no trivial matter
brings them.   The scenes around them are so ap-
propriate, so in unison with angelic appearances,
that the angels seem as natural as the golden rim
of a summer cloud.   There is nothing strained in
their introduction, nothing abrupt in their coming.
How naturally Lot's celestial visitors enter into
the tragedy of burning Sodom!   How much in
keeping with the patriarchal life of the broad free
desert are the angelic forms that adorn the story
of Abraham and Hagar and Jacob and Moses!
They are as natural as flowers blushing in the
desert air.   How inseparable they seem from the
stirring history of David and Daniel!   And in the
New Testament it is only the greatest events that
bring them out for a moment, like the invisible
electricity that flashes an instant into the summer
lightning, and sinks back into the invisible again.
We see them like the aurora shining upon the

shepherds. We see them with Zacharias and Mary. Then years pass before their burning zeal glows into visible form again. Then we see them upon the Mount of Transfiguration, in the gloom of Gethsemane, sitting on the broken tomb of the resurrection, pointing to the cloud of the ascension as it fades into the blue of heaven. That they are now invisible is no evidence that they are far away. All the greatest powers are invisible; subtile life, the enswathing air, the intangible electricity, the diligent steam, mysterious gravitation, all are invisible as the angels.

St. Luke's Day.

ST. LUKE, the beloved physician, the refined scholar, the painter of two galleries of sacred portraits — the Gospel and the Acts — was St. Paul's friend, his co-worker, his fellow-traveller, the sharer of his trials and his memories — St. Luke, the true friend. Before he was born, Cicero had written, "Friendship doubles our joys and divides our griefs." Most of that which goes by the name of friendship is as rootless as an aquatic plant, that turns its broad leaves and flowers to the summer's sun. Men desecrate the holy name of friendship by applying it to alliances, conferences, and leagues. But true friendship is one of the sweetest and best of earthly things; if, indeed, it can be called earthly. Friendship is the best developed fruit of love. It is the escape for the pent-up soul. Friends can do for each other what modesty forbids them to do for themselves. They can keep down each other's vanity, and keep up each other's courage. Friendship has the physician's skill, the nurse's vigilance, the mother's devotion. How may we procure this blessed boon? Friendship cannot be created by the jugglery of oaths and grasped hands. True friendship ought to be grounded in the love of God; it ought to be well chosen, cemented by nature and religion, developed by time, tested by adversity, consecrated by associations. Let such friendship be held at high value. Let no trivial thing imperil it. Let it be cherished by confidence unstinted, by demonstrations of affection, by sincerity and truth, by faith and trust, by mutual forbearance and sacrifice. Such friendship will be an oasis in the arid waste of selfishness; and it will be an anticipation for the life to come.

Sts. Simon and Jude's Day.

WHILE the evening hour is the holiest and the most solemn of the day, it is also often the saddest. At eventide the day is done; the books are closed; the hammer reclines on the anvil; the plough lies in the furrow; the sun is burning low in its socket; the shadows are long and ghost-like and weird; the warmth has died out of the air; the world is silent. To many a man — aye, and woman — this is a lonely hour. Separated from loved ones, welcomed by no eye, cheered by no presence, the dying embers on the hearth wave up the visions of the past, of happier days and absent forms. Sitting in the unlit gloom, the aching heart feels tears arise from it to gather in the eyes. It is then the devout soul draws near to Him who trod the wine-press alone. It is then he feels the deepest personal love for our dear Lord. It is then he most needs his sympathy. It is then he is most dependent on his companionship and communion. It is then he is most grateful for his promise, "I will never leave thee nor forsake thee."

All Saints' Day.

IN the wonderful cemetery of Père-la-Chaise in Paris, are many interesting tombs, — the tombs of Abelard and Héloise, of Molière and Racine, of Madame Rachel and Talma, of Balzac and Thiers, and the grassy grave of Marshal Ney. There is also a tomb to the unknown dead, the untombed dead. Upon this monument are hung the garlands of those who have died, whose graves they do not know or cannot reach. And this tomb is always covered with fresh flowers or immortelles.

Now I have thought that among the festivals of the Church this All Saints' Day is our monument to the unheralded dead. We have St. Peter's Day and St. John's Day and the others. But here is All Saints' Day. How many saints there have been, some known to us, who have never been nor ever will be heralded as the great of earth! Unhonored and unsung, their good deeds were interred with their bones. Stimulated by no applause and sustained by no hope of fame, they were patient in tribulation and faithful unto death. No marble marks the spot where their ashes rest. But this festival is their monument, and the prayers and praises which are offered on it are their wreaths. These lives and deaths are dear to God ; and we thank Him for the good examples of all his saints, who, having finished their course in faith, do now rest from their labors.

Ember Days.

SOME men have disbelieved Christianity because it makes the infinite God condescend to the trifles of earth. Would we discredit a biography because it described the mailed hand of a warrior rocking the cradle of a sleeping infant, or if it told of a keen critic listening with real pleasure to the broken babble of a child, or of a king who smiled at war and yet stoops to pick up his prattling tot? The king is more kingly, the critic and warrior honor themselves, by showing the paternal instinct for the tender and weak. I have seen an iron ball weighing a ton let fall a great distance upon an iron safe and crush it to pieces. But that ball was incapable of gentleness. Much more interesting and intelligent is the great steam-hammer that can strike hard enough to crush the iron safe, and can strike gently enough to drive a pin without bending it. So the blind force of blind fate, while terrible to think about, is not so great a conception as the Almighty God, who is at the same time the Almighty Father; great in the storm's blast, and gentle in the snowflake's fall; engineering the fields of heaven, staking off the stars, building the spires of grass, and coloring the forget-me-not. God is great enough to have complete control of his own greatness. God is great enough to move the whole of his infinite love down to the delicate point of sympathy that touches the heart-ache of an orphan child.

Rogation Days.

GOD always works by agents, and sends his gifts through appointed channels. By law He makes the seeds to grow, and worlds to wax and wane. The lightnings are his agents, the clouds are his channels, the fields are the tables from which He feeds the world. So in the universe of grace God works by means. By meditation the thoughts are winged from earth to heaven. By prayer the soul goes thither with the thoughts. By the Scriptures the heart is made wise. By self-examination the right road is kept, and the distance is marked. By charity life is imparted to dead faith. By the Holy Communion we feed on heavenly food, and hold high concourse with angels and archangels, and all the company of heaven. All means of grace are God-given, and all must be used. We have no right to be capricious, like children who would make a meal on sweets if we would let them. Means of grace must be used in due proportion. One may meditate too much. One may pray ineffectively. Prayer will be imperfect if unmixed with other means of grace. Without the Scriptures it will lack faith and fervor. Without self-examination it will lack aim. Without meditation it will be shallow. Without public worship it will be selfish. Without the Holy Communion its very life will be imperilled.

Thanksgiving Day.

IT is wonderful how we forget our blessings, for the simple cause that they are so constantly supplied, so abundantly given. They are common. Who thinks of being thankful for sunlight — sunlight so simple, so common, so universal? Go into Mammoth Cave and spend two or three days. It is beautiful and strange. As the chemical lights flare up at Grand Dome, or Gothic Chapel, or the Star Chamber, or Echo River, we exclaim, How beautiful, how weird, how sublime! But when the visit is over, and you come to the cavern's mouth, you are captivated by the sunlight and the colors of the world that shine and shimmer without — so brilliant, so dazzling, so gorgeous, so glorious! Bless God for the sunlight, and the green grass, and the sailing clouds, and the blue sky, so abundant, yet so good and so beautiful. Let us not fail to be mindful of blessings because they are sent to us with regularity and lavished upon us in bounty.

INDEX.